British Railways Illustrated
ANNUAL
No.5

IRWELL
PRESS

CONTENTS

SUBSCRIPTIONS
Readers can subscribe to British Railways Illustrated or its industrial/narrow gauge scion, Railway Bylines, for six or twelve issues at a time. The cost for six issues of BRILL is £15.00 inclusive of postage and packing whilst twelve issues are charged at £30.00. Bylines is bi-monthly and six issues for a year are £17.70 . Overseas subscribers should add the cost of surface/air mail. Limited numbers of back issues are also available. All remittances should be made out to IRWELL PRESS and sent to

Irwell Press General Office,
59A, High Street, Clophill,
Bedfordshire MK45 4BE
Telephone /Fax. 01525 861888
Printed & Bound by The Amadeus Press,
Huddersfield, West Yorkshire
Copyright:- Irwell Press 1996

Front cover. 45157 leaving Edinburgh Princes Street on the 4.23pm Inverness service with 45213 on Stirling a slow train in April 1960. PHOTOGRAPH Phil Lynch.
Right. E4 0-6-2T No. 32509 passing Guildford shed in May 1961. PHOTOGRAPH R.S.Greenwood
Left. West Country class No.34005 BARNSTAPLE on an Exeter bound freight west of Wilton in May 1955. PHOTOGRAPH G.F.Heiron.
Back cover. Plymouth Laira shed. PHOTOGRAPH Terry Nicholls.

Welcome to the New Revivalism - the ancient institution of the Railway Annual lives on in **British Railways Illustrated Annual No.5.** 'The Annual' is the Yuletide manifestation of the monthly magazine *British Railways Illustrated* - regular readers will know of its many 'regular' items and it is one of the joys of an Annual that a much more generous treatment is possible. One such 'bread and butter' piece from *British Railways Illustrated* - modestly referred to as *BRILL* - is **Thirties File,** greatly enlarged in this case to describe how half a million cubic yards of Essex were removed in the **Gidea Park - Shenfield Widening.** Will a railway ever be widened again in this country?

For all the vast outpouring of words concerned with our home railways over the years, the fact that so many railways abroad owed their design, construction and operation to an industry based in Britain yet *not* part of our railways, receives (relatively) scant attention. The relationship between the home commercial locomotive and equipment builders and the operating railways was an odd one. The railways built much of their own equipment and stock but were not allowed to compete directly with the commercial firms. To an extent this had the effect of robbing those firms of a sound home market, or at least a market which could be represented as such to foreign customers. British success abroad was thus an even more praiseworthy achievement. It was always said that Beyer Peacock in particular suffered from this, for there was no effective 'home stage' on which to display the attractions of the firm's articulated Garratts. If the product's that good, a foreign buyer might well ask, why don't your own railways use it? The firm's hopes for a break-through with the LMS order for Garratts in the 1930s were to be disappointed and though indeed it is very hard now to say much that is new about any important class of steam locomotive, Kevin Pile does the trick, covering well trodden (and not so well trodden) ground in **Success Abroad, Failure at Home.** D.W. Winkworth has written extensively on matters Southern and a number of his efforts have appeared in the pages of *BRILL*. **Something on Southampton** is an unusual article, a bringing together of three vastly different undertakings, built for wholly different reasons on very different scales. It brings together *Art Deco*, the embryonic BOAC, flying boats, Special Trains, an uncomfortable time for a hapless Southern Foreman and the post-War tangle of bureaucracy and material shortage.

Until well into the 1960s, Britain - England even - was a much bigger place. Not nearly so many of us had a car or access to one and even if we did, any trip other than a local one required thought and planning. A holiday really was an adventure and groaning A40s and Populars set off, *en famille*, at two o'clock in the morning as a matter of course. If congestion and the state of roads was a check on car transport the reliability of a car was always a nagging question too - no journey in the 1950s and 1960s was free of the very real possibility of breakdown. Who now carries a selection of water hoses as part of the holiday trip? Train was the way to get there but even then there was a physical landscape which had to be taken account of. There are no physical barriers to travel in Britain now. Large tracts of remoter country, well after 1945, were still served by single track roads and trains, however important, stopped *to be banked* up the difficult bits. Not only that, but Britain was such a vast wilderness that there were places where your little car was driven onto an ordinary flat wagon, to avoid a long diversion across yet another tract of country. This extraordinary place was of course the Severn Tunnel. None of these once-formidable barriers now exist - Shap has simply disappeared, whether it be for train or car and as we speed across the Severn now (or rather wait in a queue at the approaches) travellers are wholly oblivious to the old physical constraints to travel in this country. **Through the Hole** was just that.....

There was something of the *Boy's Own* about the turntable and its yard at King's Cross. The LNER, and the Eastern Region after it, knew something about advertising. The East Coast Pacifics had an allure and the Kings Cross turntable provided the perfect stage. It's a title that strains to be humorous but **On the Turn at The Cross** will bring the smile of nostalgia to any lips.

There's Bulleid Pacifics and The Red Dragon, and a smattering of *BRILL* regulars completes the Christmas treat for this year - **Diesel Dawn** sees English Electric Type 1s (then 'Type A', as the original Modernization Scheme decreed); **War Report** describes the destruction wrought on Aberdeen and the stoic 'we can take it' of the inhabitants and a couple of **Fourums** follow up with the usual mix of the sublime and ridiculous.

You'll Remember those Black & White Days...

SUCCESS ABROAD, FAILURE AT HOME
Some Notes on the LMS Garratts

Well Trodden (and not so well trodden) Ground. By Kevin Pile

It is very hard now to say much that is new about any important class of steam locomotive, but there is always room for one more outing - a different treatment and some new photographs, maybe. The story of the Garratts in England (for it was England, not Britain) is an odd one, and the first point made by most writers is that the articulated locomotive found little praise or honour in the country of its birth. The other point, again oft-made, is that despite the very

The Garratt proposals were fatally undermined, if it possible to read the corporate infighting mind all these years on, because they were identified with the losing side. George Hughes of the (brief) Horwich ascendancy had begun to look at means of ameliorating the double heading which was the curse of the Midland line coal workings to London. These were a black jewel in the crown of the vast freight operation underpinning the commercial well-being of the LMS. Both 'northern' Big Four players, the LNER and LMS, as well as the GWR, operated a vast business of (mainly

life was breathed into the project but it was Anderson, Superintendent of Motive Power, not Fowler, who liaised with Beyer Peacock.

Unfortunately the Garratts were particularly vulnerable to any ill-advised stamping of Midland 'principles'. The Garratt layout was 'Midlandised' to such an extent that the giant machines were effectively hobbled, though this was to take a time to make itself apparent. In the LMS Locomotive Committee deliberations of 17 June 1925 'three Garratt articulated Engines' were specified (for Toton - Brent as well as Toton -

Giantism - with four safety valves - comes to the county town of Yorkshire. The Garratts in later years worked on iron ore trains bound for Middlesbrough as far as York and 47977 rests there in the 1950s, an odd sight, surely, among the LNER locals. The three link couplings were specially strengthened so that they were bigger - note how in (most) photos the links are raised up, to avoid striking objects in the 'four foot'. Photograph Neville Stead Collection.

high degree of success which the Garratt designs of Beyer Peacock met across the world, at home, relatively, they were a failure.

The (literally) Achilles heel of the Garratts were the axleboxes. The Garratts were inadequately shod from the outset, due, it is said to a ill-judged attempt at 'standardisation'. It was an outcome, in part at least of bureaucratic infighting on the then youthful LMS, a giant organisation by any measure which was still in flux even as it entered its second decade, years after the Garratts had come into service.

domestic) coal to the capital, and endless trailing empties back. The only one, rather absurdly, to run this deliberately with small engines, necessitating double heading, was the Midland. Hughes' championing of any solution at this period, as Midland elements were completing an effective 'cultural take-over' of the LMS, was bound to suffer interference of some kind. The cooks, as was inevitable in these circumstances - it happens everywhere, and still does - came to spoil the broth. Hughes retired late in 1925 and the centre of things moved rapidly to Derby as Fowler took over. New

Willesden) 'to avoid the present method of double heading'. These were to have Derby short travel valves, MR type axleboxes and the 2-6-0/0-6-2 arrangement rather than Hughes' (and Beyer's) desired 2-6-2/2-6-2. All these vital differences, it is said, made for howls of anguish at Gorton. For years Beyer Peacock had wanted a home showcase for its products - now it had a hog-tied version....

These first three Garratts, 4997, 4998 and 4999, were delivered in 1927, their LMS Engine History Cards giving the 'Date Built' as 6th, 12th and 20th April respectively - pre-

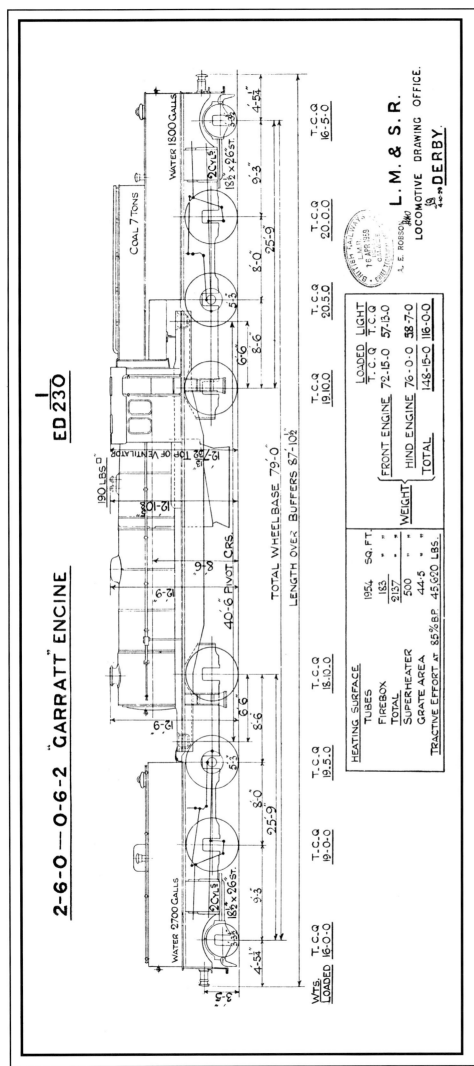

2-6-0 — 0-6-2 "GARRATT" ENGINE

$\frac{1}{ED\ 230}$

L.M. & S.R.
LOCOMOTIVE DRAWING OFFICE.
DERBY.
4-0-29

WATER 1800 GALLS
COAL 7 TONS
2 CYLS.
18½" × 26" ST.
190 LBS
12-108
TOP OF VENTILATOR
WATER 2700 GALLS
2 CYLS.
18½" × 26" ST.

TOTAL WHEEL BASE 79'-0"
LENGTH OVER BUFFERS 87'-10½"
40'-6" PIVOT CRS.

Wts.			
T.C.Q. 16-5-0			
T.C.Q. 20.0.0			
T.C.Q. 20.5.0			
T.C.Q. 19.10.0			
T.C.Q. 18.10.0			
T.C.Q. 19.5.0			
T.C.Q. 19.0.0			
LOADED 16-0-0			

WEIGHT	LOADED T.C.Q	LIGHT T.C.Q
FRONT ENGINE	72-15-0	57-13-0
HIND ENGINE	76-0-0	58-7-0
TOTAL	148-15-0	116-0-0

HEATING SURFACE		
TUBES	1954	SQ. FT.
FIREBOX	183	" "
TOTAL	2137	" "
SUPERHEATER	500	" "
GRATE AREA	44.5	" "
TRACTIVE EFFORT AT 85% B.P.	45,620 LBS.	

sumably these are the delivery dates. The cost, oddly, was not recorded, though the later, 1930, engines were given as £10,027 each. All three 1927 engines went to Toton. It has to be presumed that the later deficiencies, which can really be summed up as the inadequate axle boxes, did not immediately show to any greatly undue degree. By mid-1929 all three had managed to get well into 50,000 miles for the first heavy repair - that's over 500 miles a week. My 1950s Skool Atlas suggests Toton to be about 125 miles from north west London, which more or less amounts to a day up, a day back with empties and repeat. Since writing this I read in one eminent article that Toton lays 126½ miles from Brent - that is, Cricklewood, which says something for the pre-decimal atlas makers.

All three original Garratts stayed at Toton, according to their History Cards, until 1930, when the appearance of further engines enabled a broader disposition of these wonder machines. Apparently the loaded Toton - Brent coal trains ran to 1,500tons - 85 wagons with an equivalent 100 empties return. More than this was possible, but loops and sidings (a memory here of the problems of the giant LNER 2-8-2s) were not up to it. The Midland went to all sorts of lengths in its 'doubling up' policy, and even put in an extra column at the customary watering places, so that there was one fixed and one swinging out over the loco. These were perfectly sited for a couple of 0-6-0s and although the Garratts had tanks at each end it often took much longer to take water than before - through an oversight, Beyer Peacock had not been made aware of this system and the tank fillers did not match the columns...... At Luton for instance, watering had long been 'slick and quick' but a Garratt, with all the fiddling about, could still be there half an hour after pulling up......

On 23rd October 1929 the LMS Locomotive Committee, in Minute 893, agreed to the purchase of thirty more Garratts, at a cost of £300,000 - 'the allocation to be reported when the new engines are put into traffic.' The LMS Locomotive Committee anticipated that '68 freight tender engines' (by which, the Committee must have meant, 3F 0-6-0s) could be broken up, to 'enable a saving of £7,095 per annum.'. Each Garratt would, in essence, have freed a 4F 0-6-0, which would, through the 1930s version of what we now understand as 'cascading', replace an earlier 2F/3F or something even more humble and time-expired. It is claimed that the axlebox shortcomings were manifest from the first, but no vital modifications seem to have been incorporated in the new batch of thirty engines. Such alterations as were made were taller chimneys and domes and enlarged bunkers, changes to the ex-

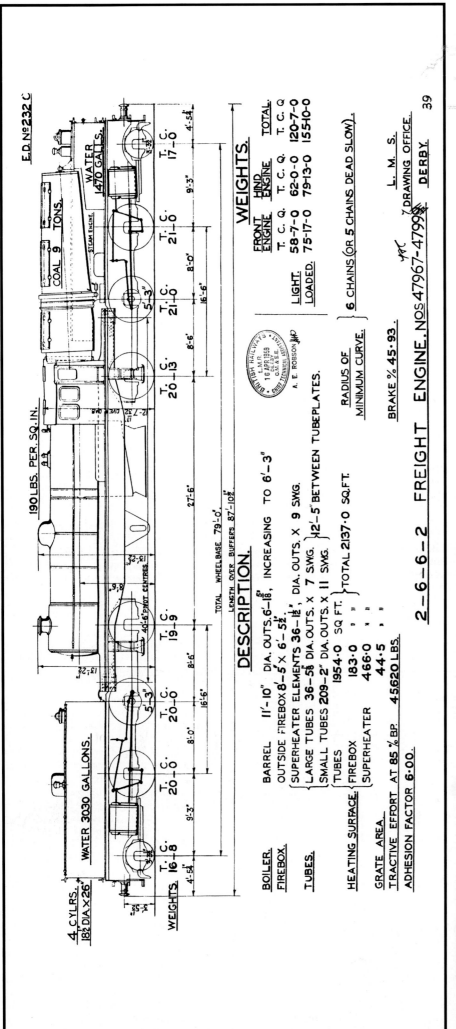

E.D. Nº 232 C

4 CYLRS. 18½" DIA × 26"

WEIGHTS.

WATER 3030 GALLONS.

COAL 9 TONS.

WATER 470 GALLS.

STEAM ENGINE.

190 LBS. PER. SQ. IN.

TOTAL WHEEL BASE 79'-0"

LENGTH OVER BUFFERS 87'-10½"

DESCRIPTION.

BOILER.	BARREL	11'-10" DIA. OUTS. 6'-1⅝", INCREASING TO 6'-3"
FIREBOX.	OUTSIDE FIREBOX 8'-5" × 6'-5½".	
TUBES.	SUPERHEATER ELEMENTS 36-1½", DIA. OUTS. × 9 SWG.	
	LARGE TUBES 36-5⅝ DIA. OUTS. × 7 SWG.	12'-5" BETWEEN TUBEPLATES.
	SMALL TUBES 209-2" DIA. OUTS. × 11 SWG.	

HEATING SURFACE.	TUBES	1954·0 SQ. FT.	TOTAL 2,137·0 SQ. FT.
	FIREBOX	183·0 " "	
	SUPERHEATER	466·0 " "	
GRATE AREA		44·5 " "	

TRACTIVE EFFORT AT 85 % B.P. 45,620 LBS.

ADHESION FACTOR 6.00.

WEIGHTS.

	FRONT ENGINE T. C. Q.	HIND ENGINE T. C. Q.	TOTAL T. C. Q.
LIGHT.	58-7-0	62-0-0	120-7-0
LOADED.	75-17-0	79-13-0	155-10-0

RADIUS OF MINIMUM CURVE. } 6 CHAINS (OR 5 CHAINS DEAD SLOW).

BRAKE % 45·93.

BRITISH RAILWAY L.M.R. 16 APR 1959 CHIEF TECHNICAL ASST. C.M. & E.E. A. E. ROBSON

L. M. S. DRAWING OFFICE DERBY

39

2-6-6-2 FREIGHT ENGINE. NOS. 47967-47999

---

haust ports and stronger frames.

One aspect of the Garratt story which has received little attention is the part they played in the initiation of the 'Repair Concentration and Garage Scheme' of 1933, which provided for works to improve the efficiency of shed operation. Minute 893, mentioned above, set out three recommendations; the first was approval of the engines followed by:

'2) That alterations be made to the layout of the yards, and wheeldrops be provided at Toton, Wellingborough and Cricklewood MPDs respectively, at a cost of £16,142.

3) That mechanical coaling and ash lifting plants be provided at Toton, Wellingborough and Cricklewood MPDs at a cost of £50,462, resulting in an annual saving of £6,071.'

Thus the advent of the Garratts played a major part in getting under way the great 1933 scheme of shed modernisation.

The Railway Gazette hailed the new order: *'Delivery of the 30 new Beyer-Garratt locomotives ordered by the LMS Railway has commenced, and the engines are, with one or two modifications, the same as the three already in service. The wheel arrangement is 2-6-0 + 0-6-2, and the advantages of a high boiler capacity, ample cylinder volume and adhesion weight are secured without overloading the track, the individual axle weights being of a moderate character, especially when the total weight of the engine is taken into account. The fact that an order of this magnitude for articulated locomotives should have been given by one of the largest railways in the world is testimony to the fact that such engines fulfil just as useful a function in normal working conditions and on well laid and, for the most part, evenly graded track as they do in what used to be termed their more*

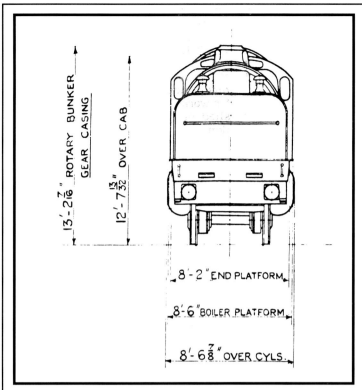

ROTARY BUNKER GEAR CASING 13'-2 7/16"

OVER CAB 12'-7 13/32"

8'-2" END PLATFORM

8'-6" BOILER PLATFORM

8'-6 7/8" OVER CYLS.

'natural' surroundings, where the conditions are of a totally different character, and curves of small radius, steep gradients and poorly-laid track combine to make the conditions of service particularly onerous and difficult to comply with. This is not, of course, to say that the work for which the new Beyer-Garratts on the LMS have been introduced is of an easy character, but rather the reverse. The point we wish to make is that whereas it is customary to work heavy freight trains in this country with what may be termed 'normal' types of engines with rigid wheel arrangements, these new articulated engines have in this case been considered superior inasmuch as they will do the work of two normal locomotives in a highly

efficient manner and with reduced coal consumption.'

This last point was fine so far as it went; the Garratts indeed replaced two locos on a train but for maintenance purposes the sheds were presented, essentially, with two 2-6-0 engines - four sets of Walschaerts valve gear, pistons, piston valves, motion and so on to look after. Only one firebox and boiler it's true but a lot bigger than a 4F....

The thirty Garratts were delivered throughout the latter part of 1930, at intervals of a few days or weeks. 'Date Built' for the first, 4968, was 16th August and 10th December for 4996, the last. 4996 by this time cost £10,414. By now the basics of winning enough coal from the cavernous bunker (a feat made worse by the sweltering conditions often experienced on board the Garratts) had prompted the LMS to try some form of coal shifting aid on the last engine. This device was described as a 'Spencer Melksham Coal Pusher'; it evidently proved inadequate and was removed, at a cost of £402 - more than it cost to fit the rotating bunker, which was £320 for each engine.

This is how the rotating bunkers came about. The first was tried out on 4986 and in July 1931 the Locomotive Committee recommended fixing new nine ton revolving bunkers to thirty of the class. This was odd. Why not all thirty-three? The trial bunker was smaller in capacity and was transferred later to one of the original three, No.4997; 4986 in replacement got one of the thirty bunkers ('self trimming' as the LMS termed them) ordered in 1931, leaving just two Garratts, 4998 and 4999, with the original square shouldered bunkers.

The 1930 batch of Garratts went to work and for the first few years managed mileages between heavy overhauls to match the first three. Some were a little under 50,000, others over 70,000, but by 1936 mileages between heavies were often under 40,000. By about 1945 figures under 20,000 were not unusual and instances of light repairs ever more frequent. It was a fairly predictable decline maybe, given the in-built faults. A drastic remedy was proposed by Beyer Peacock, that of *rebuilding* the engines to the 2-6-2+2-6-2 arrangement originally favoured by Hughes. This of course would have removed the weakness but by this time the attractions of the Garratts for the LMS, for whatever reason, had begun to pale. This reference of 9th July 1938, from the Engine History Card of 4967 records it: *'Proposal re conversion of Garratt engines from 2-6-0 to 2-6-2 wheel arrangement on each unit involving new frames, axles and axleboxes. Messrs. Beyer Peacock quotation £2,850 February 27th 1937. Estimated July 1938 price £3,500. Vice President decided no further action to be taken.'*

With this decision, the fate of the LMS Garratts was really sealed.

4997. Even early on, the locos were marked by three cleaned patches - front and rear numbers and the 'LMS' (later the BR emblem) on the cabside. The rest was a more or less uniform carpet of filth.

The true home of the Garratts was Toton; all were allocated there at one time or another and no other shed is so closely associated with them. In front is No.1 roundhouse, with Nos.2 and 3, set in line, beyond. There was no turntable in Britain which could take a Garratt and no Midland roundhouse had a long enough berth under cover. At Toton, the extraordinary step was taken of driving a road longitudinally through Nos.2 and 3 shed - see subsequent photos. Of incidental interest are: the cluster of Garratts outside No.1, a Fowler 7F 0-8-0 (another relative failure on the Midland coal workings) on the right, and the curious West Coast 'Ghost Train' rake over on the left - it existed to move coal for the LMS power station (providing third and fourth rail electricity) at Stonebridge Park in London.

There was a depreciation assessment, set at 1st January 1948, for each LMS loco, and the findings stamped on each engine's card. The first three, nominally, would have given up the ghost on their allotted 45 year span in 1972, the others in 1975. If only..... Some dates and numbers from the Engine History Cards:

First Three
4997 date built 6/4/27. **7997** 17/1/39; **47997** w.e. 8/5/48.
Transfer of self trimming bunker from 4986 31/12/32.

No.4998, one the original three and one of only two to retain the 'original' straight bunker. The first bunkers on the 'production' batch were wider, with a top slightly curved over. Cricklewood, 7 July 1930. Photograph N.E. Preedy.

47988 at Cricklewood in the 1950s. Behind is the wagon repair shop, at one time paved with wooden wagon solebars, which *retained their builders' plates*..... Readers are not advised to visit the site with metal detectors. Photograph Alec Swain.

Toton 15/11/27, **Wellingborough** 4/10/30, **Toton** 21/2/31, **Hasland** 13/8/32, **Toton** 25/11/50, **Hasland** 17/4/54, **Toton** 9/10/54, **Hasland** 6/11/54.
Collision damage 1936.
Mileage 12/36 199,519, total mileage 540,541, mileage since last General repair 28,750.

Withdrawn w.e. 11/2/56. Broken up 6/4/56.
4998 date built 12/4/27. **7998** 2/2/39; **47998** w.e. 26/3/49.
Toton 15/11/27, **Wellingborough** 4/10/30, **Toton** 21/2/31, **Westhouses** 27/4/35, **Toton** 10/2/40, **Westhouses** 8/6/40, **Toton** 29/3/41.

Mileage 12/36 199,173, total mileage 551,315, mileage since last General repair 62,410.
Withdrawn w.e. 25/8/56. Broken up 3/10/56.
4999 date built 20/4/27. **7999** 9/11/39; **47999** w.e. 22/1/49.
Toton 15/11/27, **Wellingborough** 4/10/30, **Toton** 21/2/31, **Hasland**

Garratt (doors open) under the coaling plant at Cricklewood, August 1932. 'Local' coal (rubbish) was delivered on the right and 'Main Line' (good stuff) on the left. The double roundhouse stands in the background; a few hundred yards beyond that lay the 'Brent Ash Pits' where locos had long been turned and serviced before returning north and it was there that the Garratts could be found, as often as not. There was a further peculiarity at Cricklewood, the East-West Loop which enabled engines to cross over from up to down side, passing under the main line to briefly run alongside the North Circular Road - a quite astonishing sight, I can assure anyone who has not been treated to it. (Its site, incidentally, was close to where the two Brush Type 2s 'ran over' a few years ago, an incident which found its way onto our TV sets.) The East-West Loop was one of the few places on the Midland where a Garratt *could* turn without sending it off for hours to take advantage of local junctions. It was a regular occurrence for any engine, Garratt or otherwise arriving from the north in those busy days, to use the loop to get over for servicing and to gain 'right side' for its return, conveniently turning in the process.

13/8/32, **Westhouses** 27/4/35, **Toton** 19/4/41.
Mileage 12/36 197,167, total mileage 571,909, mileage since last General repair 91,377.
Withdrawn w.e. 28/1/56. Broken up 16/3/56.

****

1930 Batch
4967 date built 21/8/30. **7967** 16/9/38; **47967** w.e. 11/12/48.
Rotating bunker 22/12/31.
Toton 6/9/30, **Westhouses** 6/4/40, **Toton** 8/6/40, **Hasland** 25/8/56.
Damaged by enemy action, Bromford Bridge near Castle Bromwich, 9/4/41.
Mileage 12/36 145,907, total mileage 592,277, mileage since last General repair 82,334.
Withdrawn w.e. 23/11/57. Broken up?
4968 date built 16/8/30. **7968** 13/6/39; **47968** w.e. 27/11/48.
Rotating bunker 24/11/31.
Toton 6/9/30, **Hasland** 28/5/38.
Mileage 12/36 133,874, total mileage 548,187, mileage since last General repair 59,170.
Withdrawn w.e. 7/9/57. Broken up?
4969 date built 24/8/30. **7969** 24/5/39; **47969** w.e. 7/8/48.
Rotating bunker 10/11/31.
Toton 6/9/30, **Hasland** 25/2/56.
Mileage 12/36 152,582, total mileage 579,671, mileage since last General repair 70,941.
Withdrawn w.e. 3/8/57. Broken up 5/10/57.
4970 date built 27/8/30. **7970**?; **47970** w.e. 14/5/49.
Rotating bunker 17/11/31.
Toton 6/9/30.
Mileage 12/36 154,587, total mileage 559,577, mileage since last General repair 63,200.
Withdrawn w.e. 2/7/55. Broken up 5/8/55.
4971 date built 30/8/30. **7971** 3/9/38; **47971** w.e. 30/10/48.
Rotating bunker 29/10/31.
Toton 6/9/30, **Hasland** 15/2/41, **Toton** 17/4/54, **Hasland** 21/1/56.
Mileage 12/36 145,554, total mileage - not recorded - mileage at 31/12/50 443,871, mileage since last General repair - not recorded.
Withdrawn w.e. 10/11/56. Broken up 18/1/57.
4972 date built 5/9/30. **7972** 2/3/39; **47972** w.e. 26/6/48.
Rotating bunker 30/11/31.
Toton 6/9/30, **Hasland** 24/3/56.
Mileage 12/36 154,527, total mileage 588,101, mileage since last General repair 66,008.
Withdrawn w.e. 6/4/57. Broken up 3/5/57.
4973 date built 6/9/30. **7973** 16/8/38; **47973** w.e. 5/2/49.
Rotating bunker 31/12/31.
Toton 6/9/30, **Hasland** 1/10/38.
Mileage 12/36 159,277, total mileage 574,087, mileage since last General repair 64,086.
Withdrawn w.e. 13/4/57. Broken up 6/7/57.

47971 at Toton, 24 July 1955. It stands alongside Nos.2 and 3 sheds, and the entrance to the long 'Garratt Road' can be seen at the left. The coal needs to be trimmed to enable bunker the doors to be closed - a preparation job for the fireman. Photograph Brian Morrison.

4974 date built 2/9/30. **7974** 11/4/39; **47974** w.e. 4/9/48.
Rotating bunker 8/1/32.
Toton 6/9/30, **Wellingborough** 24/2/51, **Toton** 20/11/54.
Mileage 12/36 174,306, total mileage 601,260, mileage since last General repair 96,486.
Withdrawn w.e. 26/5/56. Broken up 24/7/56.
4975 date built 18/9/30. **7975** 11/1/39; **47975** w.e. 12/6/48.
Rotating bunker 29/12/31.
Toton 4/10/30.
Mileage 12/36 168,474, total mileage 563,852, mileage since last General repair 100,183.
Withdrawn w.e. 2/7/55. Broken up 26/8/55.
4976 date built 20/9/30. **7976** 29/9/39; **47976** w.e. 6/11/48.

Rotating bunker 15/12/31.
Toton 4/10/30.
Mileage 12/36 171,907, total mileage 574,688, mileage since last General repair 46,825.
Withdrawn w.e. 24/3/56. Broken up 15/6/56.
4977 date built 22/9/30. **7977** 30/9/39; **47977** w.e. 11/9/48.
Rotating bunker 15/1/32.
Toton 4/10/30, **Wellingborough** 24/2/51, **Toton** 20/11/54, **Hasland** 11/12/54.
Mileage 12/36 162,509, total mileage 563,552, mileage since last General repair 68,007.
Withdrawn w.e. 17/6/56. Broken up 14/8/56.
4978 date built 24/9/30. **7978** 22/11/38; **47978** w.e. 13/11/48.

Rotating bunker 13/1/32.
Toton 4/10/30, **Hasland** 17/4/54.
Mileage 12/36 146,776, total mileage 576,633, mileage since last General repair 92,386.
Withdrawn w.e. 16/3/57. Broken up 5/4/57.
4979 date built 26/9/30. **7979** 27/2/39; **47979** w.e. 5/6/48.
Rotating bunker 17/12/31.
Toton 4/10/30, **Hasland** 25/8/56.
Mileage 12/36 167,473, total mileage 603,428, mileage since last General repair 89,275.
Withdrawn w.e. 2/2/57. Broken up 19/3/57.
4980 date built 30/9/30. **7980** 9/7/39; **47980** w.e. 2/10/48.
Rotating bunker 19/1/32.
Toton 4/10/30, **Hasland** 28/5/38.

Mileage 12/36 147,846, total mileage 566,639, mileage since last General repair 58,186.
Withdrawn w.e. 9/2/57. Broken up 1/3/57.
4981 date built 2/10/30. **7981** 27/8/38; **47981** w.e. 19/2/49.
Rotating bunker 19/2/32.
Toton 4/10/30.
Mileage 12/36 142,951, total mileage 569,078, mileage since last General repair 60,989.
Withdrawn w.e. 3/11/56. Broken up ?
4982 date built 7/10/30. **7982** 24/10/38; **47982** w.e. 18/9/48.
Rotating bunker 9/10/31.
Toton 1/11/30 (period ending), **Wellingborough** 24/2/51, **Toton** 20/11/54, **Hasland** 11/12/54.
Mileage 12/36 160,550, total mileage

606,777, mileage since last General repair 69,300.
Withdrawn w.e. 14/12/57. Broken up ?
4983 date built 9/10/30. **7983** 15/11/38; **47983** w.e. 9/10/48.
Rotating bunker 2/2/32.
Cricklewood 1/11/30 (period ending), **Toton** 27/12/30 (period ending), **Hasland** 28/5/38.
Mileage 12/36 148,095, total mileage 546,602, mileage since last General repair 87,962.
Withdrawn w.e. 14/1/56. Broken up 2/3/56.
4984 date built 11/10/30. **7984** 10/10/38; **47984** w.e. 26/6/48.
Rotating bunker 24/12/31.
Cricklewood 1/11/30 (period ending), **Wellingborough** 2/32, **Hasland** 8/32, **Toton** 17/4/54.

A quite wonderful view of a Garratt, highlighting the extraordinary length of the things. Presumed to be Toton, with the Garratt on a run round line.

Mileage 12/36 144,714, total mileage 539,038, mileage since last General repair 45,470.
Withdrawn w.e. 25/2/56. Broken up 23/3/56.
4985 date built 15/10/30. **7985** 5/6/39; **47985** w.e. 22/5/48.
Rotating bunker 27/1/32.

Cricklewood 1/11/30 (period ending), **Wellingborough** 2/32, **Toton** 13/8/32.
Mileage 12/36 148,943, total mileage 540.541, mileage since last General repair 76,386.
Withdrawn w.e. 11/6/55. Broken up 2/7/55.

4986 date built 13/11/30. **7986** 1/5/39; **47986** w.e. 25/9/48.
Rotating bunker 29/1/32.
Wellingborough 29/11/30, **Toton** 12/32, **Wellingborough** 12/12/53, **Hasland** 20/11/54.
Mileage 12/36 145,641, total mileage 588,916, mileage since last General repair 49,291.
Withdrawn w.e. 10/7/57. Broken up 30/8/57.
4987 date built 17/10/30. **7987** 6/12/38; **47987** w.e. 15/1/49.
Rotating bunker 13/11/31.
Collision damage 1/35.
Wellingborough 1/11/30 (period ending), **Toton** 10/10/36, **Hasland** 6/4/57.
Mileage 12/36 122,674, total mileage 554,637, mileage since last General repair 61,908.
Withdrawn w.e. 4/5/57. Broken up 24/5/57.
4988 date built 22/10/30. **7988** 4/3/39; **47988** w.e. 25/12/48.
Rotating bunker 11/12/31.
Wellingborough 1/11/30 (period ending), **Toton** 10/10/36, **Wellingborough** 12/12/53, **Toton** 8/5/54, **Hasland** 7/1/56.
Mileage 12/36 112,973, total mileage 528,224, mileage since last General repair 74,308
Withdrawn w.e. 18/8/56. Broken up 18/9/56.
4989 date built 25/10/30. **7989** 4/10/38; **47989** w.e. 2/7/49.
Rotating bunker 5/11/31.
Wellingborough 1/11/30 (period ending), **Toton** 10/10/36.
Mileage 12/36 132,808, total mileage 533,531, mileage since last General repair 87,899.

Saltley, with 47998 (screw coupling on this one), 30 January 1955. Photograph P.W. Shuttleworth.

Wellingborough shed yard, August 1954. There was a peculiar derailment of a Garratt on the Midland, which further emphasised the specific difficulties - of weight and size - they could cause. The Garratt was on down empties near Sandridge when a bad hot box was observed. It was decided to 'knock out' the offending vehicle at Sandridge. The Garratt had to venture well into the siding with the front part of the train and the tired old ash ballast, typical of such a siding, simply couldn't take the strain. The track just 'spread' below the weight and rigid wheelbase and one 'unit' descended slowly into the 'four foot'. St Albans gang with their van could not cope with this and the Cricklewood crane and gang, which didn't normally venture that far, had to assist. The engine had to be jacked up, track gauge restored by adjustable tie-bars, then lowered down. The rear half of the train, stranded on the Down Slow, was rescued by the resident St Albans Jocko 3F tank. Photograph Peter Groom.

Withdrawn w.e. 12/11/55. Broken up 18/5/56.
4990 date built 30/10/30. **7990** 28/12/38; **47990** w.e. 1/5/48.
Rotating bunker 27/11/31.
Wellingborough 1/11/30 (period ending), **Toton** 10/10/36, **Hasland** 29/3/41, Toton 17/4/54.
Mileage 12/36 130,878, total mileage

489,585, mileage since last General repair 86,131.
Withdrawn w.e. 28/5/55. Broken up 1/7/55.
4991 date built 31/10/30. **7991** 21/8/39; **47991** w.e. 28/8/48.
Rotating bunker 18/12/31.
Wellingborough 1/11/30 (period ending), **Toton** 11/8/34.

Mileage 12/36 144,329, total mileage 549,333, mileage since last General repair 79,247.
Withdrawn w.e. 31/12/55. Broken up 24/2/56.
4992 date built 4/11/30. **7992** 31/1/39; **47992** w.e. 19/6/48.
Rotating bunker 20/11/31.
Wellingborough 29/11/30, **Toton**

Garratts got to Gloucester, even at a very late date - this is 47972 on 22 October 1955. The Garratts could be thoroughgoing nuisances at sheds, through their inconvenient size. If something unfortunate happened at an outpost like this then a wheelset, say, could be taken out in the wheel drop (the humble corrugated shelter beyond) and the loco set aside in the normal course of things. A Garratt, however, could not be got properly under cover except on the 'back road'. It would be run over the turntable straight onto the exit road beyond and be left standing only *partly* under cover - always assuming it was the right way round for the end you needed to work on. This, after all, was all they could do at Hasland, which had a permanent allocation! At Cricklewood the Garratts were even more inconvenient - straightforward brake adjustment required each unit in turn over a pit. The engines usually stood in the doorway of No.1 shed, stopping all other movements. No wonder they did not stay long on the 14A allocation.... Photograph P.W. Shuttleworth.

4995 at Wellingborough, 3 September 1933. Here, facilities of a sort were created by giving over the ancient MR ground level coal shed for the Garratts. Photograph H.C. Casserley.

10/10/36, **Hasland** 29/3/41.
Mileage 12/36 109,446, total mileage 498,820, mileage since last General repair 58,416.
Withdrawn w.e. 10/3/56. Broken up 26/6/56.
4993 date built 7/11/30. **7993** 8/8/39; **47993** w.e. 24/4/48.
Rotating bunker 3/12/31.
Wellingborough 29/11/30, **Toton** 10/10/36, **Hasland** 29/3/41, **Toton** 7/11/53, **Hasland** 17/4/54.
Mileage 12/36 136,733, total mileage 555,505, mileage since last General repair 58,718.

Withdrawn w.e. 31/12/55. Broken up 3/2/56.
4994 date built 11/11/30. **7994** 27/3/39; **47994** w.e. 16/4/49.
Rotating bunker 15/2/32.
Wellingborough 29/11/30, **Toton** 10/10/36, **Wellingborough** 24/2/51, **Toton** 20/11/54, **Hasland** 8/12/56.
Mileage 12/36 129,654, total mileage 584,200, mileage since last General repair 68,270.
Withdrawn w.e. 29/3/58. Broken up ?
4995 date built 19/11/30. **7995** 28/4/39; **47995** w.e. 9/4/49.
Rotating bunker 5/1/32.

Wellingborough 29/11/30, **Toton** 10/10/36, **Wellingborough** 24/2/51, **Toton** 20/11/54, **Hasland** 6/4/57.
Mileage 12/36 131,921, total mileage 586,754, mileage since last General repair 53,834.
Withdrawn w.e. 6/7/57. Broken up 9/8/57.
4996 date built 10/12/30. **7996** 20/2/39; **47996** w.e. 11/6/49.
Rotating bunker and removal of Spencer Melksham Coal Pusher 22/1/32.
Wellingborough 27/12/30, **Toton** 10/10/36.
Mileage 12/36 127,111, total mileage

That wonderful side view. 4999 at Toton, 16 June 1928. Photograph H.C. Casserley.

Garratt on the move. 47996 on the Midland main line in Hertfordshire (I think - doubtless readers will soon put me right) with a wonderful collection of wooden mineral wagons. The Midland main line was something of a switchback, so much so that a long coal train could be sitting on two or three gradients at the same time. Drivers and guards had to develop a high degree of skill and finesse in handling such trains, to avoid 'snatches' and consequent breakage of couplings.

4987 at Cricklewood, 22 April 1934. Behind it is another Garratt. Up to a dozen or more of the big engines could end up at Cricklewood of a weekend, coaled and ready to return north from the Monday on. The Garratts could 'fail' for an unusual reason; the bunker could revolve a mite too far and then jam, full. The shed yard would echo with curses and the ring of hammer blows as all available staff were rounded up to empty it and get the thing moving. This was no joke with a nine ton capacity tender.... Photograph Harold James.

'mileages since last General repair' obviously needs to be treated with some caution. There was always an element of fiddling in mileage returns, particularly if a 'clapper' needed its life extended to keep the actuaries happy. In the 1930s, a figure of 55,000 would be about right for a Garratt 'since last heavy repair' and by the 1950s a figure in excess of 30,000 seemed to be fairly good going. So all of the 'final' figures above represent a considerable extension of each engine's 'natural'. This is nothing extraordinary of course; the London Midland 1956 'Condemning Programme', which came into effect from 1st January that year meant that the authorities had condemned all the Garratts in 1955. Only minimum expenditure would be authorised after that and as the engines staggered through 1956 and 1957, they were reduced to ever more local and easier work. Week after week out of steam doubtless went down in the record as 'local' and up and up the last

534,035, mileage since last General repair 100,879.
Withdrawn w.e. 9/6/56. Broken up 3/8/56.

****

The above details are culled from the Engine History Cards and they need to be looked at with some care. There are some problems of interpretation and the precise system of recording changed over the years, with different emphasis on practice, and with different generations of clerks filling in the forms. Still, they give a fairly comprehensive picture - they are not tablets of stone, however, and as long as they not regarded as the 'last word' it is possible to present a reasonable 'life history' of each engine. The note

Out of Traffic	To Traffic	Repair Class.	Since previous General or Intermediate
25/2/51	9/4/51	LC	6,217
21/1/52	28/2/52	LI	23,584
20/5/53	6/7/53	HI	28,556
28/12/53	21/1/54	LC*	11,392
21/9/54	5/11/54	HG	27,714
24/9/55	19/11/55	LI	22,913

LC=Light Casual, LI=Light Intermediate, HI=Heavy Intermediate, HG=Heavy General. All repairs at Crewe, except*, which is recorded as 'shed' repair.

Garratt after a bash. The number and the occasion is unrecorded on Harold James' original print but it's almost certainly 4997, after its contretemps of 1936. With all that in front of the cab it was difficult to judge distances, especially on a curve.

On the job at Trent Junction, November 1956. To reach London, or to get back to the Midlands without breaking a coupling required care and familiarity with all the vagaries of the up and down route. The secret was to keep the couplings taut to avoid the 'snatches' that put the final, fatal strain on a coupling. At Luton for instance, there is a dip south of the station. A Garratt on a down empties had, unusually, stopped for water and took its customary age to fill up (the tanks were connected by an oh so slow equilibrium pipe); the guard had not screwed his brake on to keep the couplings taut through the dip, so the rear wagons were buffered up. The engine started off north in fine fashion, but the almighty wrench to the couplings broke the last one, leaving the van behind. The guard laid detonators to protect the lost van and the Luton Jocko, No.7261, a 3F 0-6-0T, had to go south to Chiltern Green, to cross over and run back to propel the van to its train, by now stopped at Leagrave to await events.

heroic mileages went. 47995's last years were fairly typical *(See left)*.

The Garratts had a series of minor modifications (the first three had 'food boxes' added among other things, presumably to conform with the later batch of thirty); some cards list this work in detail, some cards show no such work at all. 47983 (as 4983) has the following, fairly typical, details appended:
Relief valves fitted.
Brake hanger carrier.
Brake shaft carrier brackets.
New chimney.
Ashpan door bolts in place of rivets.
New steel axleboxes.
New type frame keeps.

New type spring hanger.
Axlebox dust shields.
Axlebox oil pad.
Protection plate for pivot centre trailing unit.
Additional fixing for footplate mounting.
Strengthening frame plates.

47999 at Toton. Firing the Garratts was no sinecure, even with the revolving bunkers, for the heat could be ferocious. Unusually, the fireman could often be found wearing *gloves,* something quite out of the ordinary in LMR practice at that time - though it was later often seen on BR Standards with wide fireboxes. Photograph Neville Stead Collection.

47968 rests at York, presumably after running in a load of iron ore for Middlesbrough. Photograph Neville Stead Collection.

Apart from brief spells at Cricklewood and Westhouses for one or two, the Garratts lived out their lives at three sheds, Toton, Wellingborough and Hasland. All three places were devoted to the movement of coal and iron ore and little else, and the Garratts slogged out the years on the Midland main line. As well as Brent, they got to Willesden (as the Locomotive Committee had originally intended - see text) across on the line from Market Harborough to Northampton. Their wider sphere of activity included Toton - Birmingham Washwood Heath, Cudworth, Normanton, Staveley and Rugby, and to Peterborough, Gloucester and even Bristol. Hasland iron ore jobs took them to York and to Gowhole.

The last Garratt went in March 1958. 47994 was the only one to work into 1958 and *The London Midland Magazine* recorded a brief Obituary: '*The Garratts worked coal Toton - Brent, minerals in the Erewash valley and between Avenue Sidings near Chesterfield and Gowhole, near New Mills. 47994 was latterly used on local freight between Avenue Sidings and Toton.*'

I'd like to express my grateful thanks to Stephen Summerson and Alec Swain in the preparation of this article. Whilst any errors that remain are mine, consulting these very Midland gentlemen reassures me no end.

47974 at Toton, on the roads customarily devoted to the Garratts, alongside Nos.2 and 3 roundhouses. If the Garratts could be fearsome to work, in sometimes insufferable heat, there were compensations. Swung, effectively, between two bogies, they enjoyed almost coach-like riding qualities. They had, in the not-too serious footplate parlance of the time, 'limousine cabs'. Photograph Neville Stead Collection.

4977 at Crewe, in for repair at an unrecorded date. Photograph Neville Stead Collection.

47979, one set of doors open, at Toton. Mr D.R. Carling (he helped re-erect them at Derby) wrote an account of the LM Garratts in *Railway World*, July 1984, making the fascinating point that, though Beyer Peacock was apprised of what was expected of the locos in respect of curvature (5 chains on the main line) no-one told them about the 3$\frac{1}{2}$ chains to be encountered in the Derby Works yard, or the extreme *vertical* curvature at the Toton hump. It was the custom for engines to stop and help push the preceding train over the hump and as the first Garratt went over, chimney first, the leading wheels lifted off and the leading unit tilted. Outer and inner coupled wheelsets lifted off the rails so that the leading unit was carried for a moment by its *driving axle* only, a potentially disastrous outcome repeated as the rear unit came over the hump. The inner coupled wheels, the writer reports, came through the cab floor! By some great good chance, Mr Carling records, the whole show stayed on the rails. The axleload of some 65 tons must have damaged the axleboxes and probably the frames too - the hump had to be 'smoothed out' and spaces made in the cab floors for future Garratt operation. Photograph Neville Stead Collection.

Above. 47991, July 1955. Photograph Brian Morrison.

Below. Inside Toton Nos.2 and 3 roundhouses - a perfect illustration of how the buildings were converted to house the Garratts, July 1955. The conventional engine on the left is standing on a radiating stall which, with the other roads on this side, have been cut back. Some of the roads were reduced to such an extent that only a small tank engine could be accommodated. Photograph Brian Morrison.

Above. Toton, with 47981 outside the 'Garratt Road' at the back of No.3 roundhouse. The conventional entrance to the shed (leading to the turntable) lies out of sight behind the engine, under the centre roof pitch, and is betrayed by the smoke-blackened brickwork. Photograph Neville Stead Collection.

Below. No.47994, brooding at Hasland. Many of the Garratts figured at some time on the allocation of this strangely atmospheric, strangely isolated shed. However, Toton and Wellingborough were considered their true homes, and only at those sheds were any special attempts made to cater for them. Hasland saw so many of the class on its official complement only because it was convenient for a number to see out their days there, winding up those enormous final mileages on local goods. The only place a Garratt could be housed at Hasland was on the 'back road', driven across the turntable and left with part of it poking out the rear entrance. This practice continued even after most of the shed roof was removed in consequence of subsidence! Photograph Neville Stead Collection.

47973 in Crewe Works yard, May 1957. It had 'come home' for scrapping and languished there for another few weeks before being broken up. The Garratts were assigned to Crewe for repairs and all were scrapped there, except for one, stranded by a drivers' strike and cut up at Derby. Photograph Peter Ward.

4981. The front tank was half as large again as the rear tank, and had the situation with respect to the twin columns on the Midland been conveyed to the manufacturers, doubtless the fillers at each end could have been matched to the columns, so that both could be used at the same time. The problem was compounded because drivers, unfortunately, were habituated to the smaller rear tank, which only meant the *lower* part of the front tank being filled.... No wonder there were complaints of delays whilst watering. On the second batch of thirty the problem was made even worse by raising and enlarging the front tank, to allow for the extra two tons of coal.

Below. Garratt on the go. 47974 on an up mineral passing the station platforms at Luton, prior to stopping for water. When gently restarting the train down the grade to tighten the couplings, the exhaust could be seen as quick pairs of puffs, due to the different lengths of the exhaust passages to the blast pipe. When the engine was opened up, this disappeared, becoming a very woolly 'woof'. If one end slipped.... well, a 'bass bellow' hardly describes a sound that could only have been a Garratt.

Above. 4991 near Elstree, with the usual haul of coal wagons disappearing into the distance. Mr S.T. Yaxley wrote to *Trains Illustrated* in 1959, recalling the undulating nature of the Midland main line and the problems it posed for the integrity of the train. There were *six* 'divisions' recorded on one day alone and tests instituted to obtain data, on which some kind of working practice could be based. The driver was encouraged to do exactly what he was accustomed to do, but not a single 'break' occurred....

Below. Be-hankerchiefed fireman on 47974. D.R. Carling in his marvellous *Railway World* piece reveals that (as far as he saw) there was no attempt at all to inculcate any particular way of working into the crews on the Garratts. There was no extra information for these very different machines and no running inspectors went out on the new engines. That's the way it was.....

Above. The Railway Show has declined now almost to vanishing point - BR or whatever your local bit of railway is now called simply doesn't have all those useful yards to display the stuff anymore. One of the most memorable exhibitions was the one at Marylebone Goods Yard in 1961, some exhibits of which have already featured in these columns. It was a fine display of all that was up to the minute and marks, maybe, the last time in which British Railways was prepared to present steam as any sort of contender in the motive power stakes. Soon after this, steam locos were an embarrassment only talked about in terms of how soon their elimination would be accomplished. The most startling exhibit must have been GT3 - a sight indeed sandwiched between (what is assumed to be) the 1J tender of DUKE OF GLOUCESTER and E3059, another modern locomotive built in 1961.

Below. The other Duke at Marylebone was the Duke of Edinburgh. 92220 EVENING STAR (incredibly only a year younger than GT3 and E3059) forms a backdrop to what was doubtless a memorable day for this BR man.

Above. A curious picture, taken it is said, in December 1948. The cab is a mock-up but of quite what is not clear. The location is given as 'the School on Wheels at St Enoch Station'. This explains some of the curious features at the periphery of the view - *A Reader Writes* in the monthly parent magazine of this *Annual* will no doubt carry an explanation soon.....

Left. More royalty - all part of the editor's campaign for elevation to the peerage. This apparently is the coach used by Queen Alexandra in 1903, on show at an exhibition of British royal trains at Battersea Wharf station near Chelsea Bridge, in June 1953. Now *that* is a sleeping compartment.

PICKING UP THE MAIL

A Ringside Seat by J.L. Stevenson

From early days I was fascinated by descriptions of the collection and delivery of mailbags at speed using the lineside apparatus. Imagination was further fired by illustrations in the Bassett-Lowke catalogue of their Gauge O mail van and accompanying ground equipment. But at something like a fiver such capital outlay was well beyond my meagre financial resources, and fairy godmothers/rich aunts were in extremely short supply. So, some forty years later in September 1966 I leapt at the suggestion by Dugald Cameron that we should nip up to Larbert in time for the Aberdeen - Carstairs portion of the West Coast Postal. He too admitted that such operations were of great interest to him and offered me a lift in his sports car.

The lineside apparatus in question was located about 1¼ miles south of Larbert station between Larbert Junction and Carmuirs West Junction signal boxes, just north of the bridge over the A803. So, setting out from Glasgow shortly after 17.00 we arrived on the scene in nice time for the 15.30 from Aberdeen. In due course the postman arrived carrying two heavy bags, no doubt bearing a substantial portion of the literary output from the FK district. We had expected that he

would express some disquiet at the sight of the pair of us loafing around but he greeted us as if an interested presence was both usual and acceptable. We did in fact have lineside photographic permits in these happy and enlightened days.

The accompanying photographs depict the course of events:-

The apparatus in the normal position with the projecting arms swung clear, awaiting the arrival of the GPO.

Postman arrived and lugs the bags up to the intermediate platform, ready to be suspended on one of the arms. One bag is now hooked on.

Preparations are suspended when the Larbert Junction signalman rings to say that he is sending through a light engine. Class 5 No.45029 passes en route for Motherwell.

The bags are mounted side by side on one of the arms, and swung out into the delivery position. The lower parts of the bags are secured by light string to the standard (presumably to prevent their being dragged forward by the slipstream of the train).

His rebus confectis (as Caesar would have said) we set off for home, Cameron, *alias* Jim Clark, making excellent time along the A80. Perhaps it was the proximity of my bottom to the road in the sports car which caused me to feel queasy and/or the sight of buses and lorries towering above but whatever it was, as we approached Glasgow I felt that a state of emergency was not far distant. So I suggested that a visit to Eastfield MPD might prove profitable. A scout around the shed pulled me round, though one was scarcely inspired by the sight of a Standard Class 5 No.73095 from foreign parts withdrawn and looking very sorry for itself. That apart it was a memorable and very enjoyable trip for which I must again give grateful thanks to Dugald.

Above. All is ready; the Larbert Junction starting signal goes to the off position as does the Carmuirs West distant beneath it. We wait tensely.

Below. The train, Class 5 hauled, passes at speed. The bags are collected in a flash and fall into the van.

On the Turn

These columns have touched several times on the particular interest of Kings Cross as a terminus. Few, if any, were better for 'platform ending', for the locomotive yard was only a few feet away, and a source of constant noise and activity. Even in diesel days there were plenty of engine movements - they could have even increased, for Top Shed, beyond the yawning tunnels, was closed and a servicing depot erected on the old loco yard, for diesel examination. A fuelling point replaced the old coaling plant and of course, the turntable was taken out. More than thirty years on, 'The Cross' is a shadow of its former self and the loco yard a rubbish and rubble-strewn waste. Traces of the 'table pit are still there however, and only this (together, maybe, with the long blocked-up doorway at the top of the high embankment in Goods Way) remain to suggest what wonders had once gone on. This is FLYING SCOTSMAN in the days when it had a corridor tender, on the Kings Cross turntable.

at The Cross

A view to show the lay of the land, how the loco yard related to the terminus. Running across the top of Gas Works Tunnel is Goods Way, a thoroughfare now of evil repute. The Great Northern had begun attempts to buy the site before 1914 ('a defunct gasworks'); the third Gas Works Tunnel (the one on the left) had opened in 1892 and the ground needed for the loco yard was held back by a high wall. The yard eventually opened for use, with its turntable, in 1924. Observe the height of Goods Way and the new shallow cutting on the far left - it is clear that an awful lot of earth had to be shifted. This view is dated 29 April 1952.

The loco yard from the west, with Goods Way and the buildings of the great goods depot beyond. The pointed structure is familiar to all local denizens - named 'the Ebonite Tower' after the advertising it carried, it was actually a factory chimney. 10 January

A view which completes our look at the yard from (more or less) all possible angles - this time from Goods Way. QUICKSILVER is leaving past B1 No. 61207, probably the main line pilot. This is where the pilot stood, anyway, crewed by Top Link men. These would be on a 'rest week', which was a way of evening up the mileage rates. 21 August 1956.

SUN CASTLE close up, viewed from the cutting. A variety of engines used the 'bottom loco', including some of the N2s for a bit of a clean up. Frequently junior Kings Cross men brought engines from the platform end, allowing visiting crews to book off, take tea and so on. A delightfully innocent tract of 1951, *Your British Railways*, had a similar picture, entitled *'Oh! So Easy. Modern turntables are worked from the locomotive's own brake pump. A simple connection and the job is done without any effort. Before, the driver and fireman had themselves to push the whole turntable and its hundred-ton load round.'* The 'bottom shed' 'table was indeed regarded as an easy one, in quite some contrast to one at Top Shed.

The nitty-gritty. The great table itself, occupied by New England's SUN CASTLE. It had the doubtful distinction of being one of only a few locos for which enginemen habitually used its name. It was of course, the usual affectionate Mickey-take, in this case slightly obscene.... A stamped addressed envelope (plain brown) and a promise not to reveal the contents to the Editor will secure the said epithet.

SUN CASTLE, providing that classic Kings Cross vista, which photographers back to the earliest *Boys Book of Trains* found irresistible. The yard at Kings Cross operated much after the fashion of that other great London terminus yard, at Ranelagh Bridge outside Paddington. Engines from further off ran back to Top Shed for attention, while the yard served mainly for engines from sheds closer to home - usually south of Doncaster.

FOURUM
Shed bashing - *Bylines* style

Above. As BRILL regulars will already know, our sister magazine, RAILWAY BYLINES, concentrates on minor, industrial and light railways. BRILL regulars will also know that, in these hallowed pages, no opportunity is missed to spread word of our sibling. This is such an opportunity - possibly worthy of a title along the lines of 'The Ones Aidan Fuller Forgot'. Aidan Fuller was, of course, the creator of the celebrated *British Locomotive Shed Directory* , the essential guide for all those who enjoyed a good shed bash. But BR - or Aidan Fuller - didn't have a monopoly on engine sheds. There were *other* sheds - the sort of premises which were to be found on industrial systems throughout Britain. The sort of premises which, in fact, are the proverbial magnet for RAILWAY BYLINES. Of all the industrial railway engine sheds in Britain, among the most charismatic were those of the Padarn Railway, the famous 1ft 10³/₄ in-gauge system which served the Dinorwic slate quarries in North Wales. The quarries were split into various levels (or galleries, as they were known) and one or more locomotives worked on each one. Railway operations on each gallery were fairly self-contained, due principally to the logistical problems of movement between them - this was by means of cable-worked inclines and so, once an engine was ensconced on its gallery, it would change location only when absolutely necessary. There was an engine shed on each gallery, and as locomotives remained at their allotted workplace for anything up to fifteen years (or sometimes more!) continuously, the sheds had to undertake all types of repairs, even boiler changes. The shed pictured here is, in fact, the one at Lernion gallery - at 1,860ft above sea level, the highest engine shed in Britain. The locomotive is RED DAMSEL, a Hunslet 0-4-0ST (W/No.493) of 1889. Photograph dated 26 August 1954.

Below. Many of the ironstone quarry workings in the East Midlands eventually became part of the Stewarts & Lloyds empire. One such cluster of workings was Finedon Quarries, which were connected to Wellingborough Ironworks by a metre gauge railway. One of the engine sheds was at Wellingborough, where S&L No.85, a Peckett 'M7' class 0-6-0ST (W/No.1870 of 1934), was photographed taking on water on 18 August 1966. At this time, the local council had already acquired much of the land for redevelopment, and the celebrated railway system - the very last steam-worked metre gauge line in ironstone country - was soon to close.
PHOTOGRAPH: K.C.H. FAIREY

Above. Many industrial engine sheds were, shall we say, somewhat rustic, but that, maybe, only added to their charm. This structure - call it rustic, workaday or whatever - stood adjacent to Sittingbourne Mill, at the southern end of Messrs. Bowater's 2ft 6in gauge system, which connected the mill to Ridham Dock, on the River Swale. The locomotive is Kerr Stuart 0-4-2ST LEADER (W/No.926 of 1906), and the date is 14 May 1960. PHOTOGRAPH: R.C. RILEY

Below. For some eighty years or so, Dagenham Dock did good business. Throughout its operational life, it was privately owned by Messrs. Samuel Williams & Sons. The Williams concern was impressively self-sufficient, having its own ships, barges, road transport, standard gauge railway system, locomotives and workshops - by the 1950s the firm's shipping operations had contracted a little, but the company still employed, directly or indirectly, over 1,000 people. At that time no less than 22 miles of railway track was in daily use at the Williams premises, worked by a fleet of six steam engines and four diesels. Seen outside the Williams engine shed on 9 March 1957 was Manning Wardle 0-6-0ST No.1 (W/No.1590 of 1903) and, behind it, Hudswell Clarke 0-6-0ST No.10 (W/No.1526 of 1924) in the curious duck egg blue livery. On the left, Barclay 0-6-0ST No.12 (W/No.1129 of 1907) rests inside the annexe. PHOTOGRAPH: R.C. RILEY

Above. 70024 VULCAN slips violently in the wet, starting the up Red Dragon out of Newport in May 1958. It retains the original handrails on the smoke deflectors, despite the Milton accident on home ground in 1955, which led to grab holes and cut outs on many engines.

Below. Doubtless the 165 minute journey time, despite its length, would surpass in comfort anything on offer in speedier years - look how *inviting* those compartments are at Paddington in the early 1950s. The Red Dragon came up from Wales as the 8.45am off Swansea and the down working left Paddington at 5.55pm. It would deposit you at Carmarthen at five minutes to midnight.. Don't you *yearn* to be on it?

Here Be Dragons

Photographs by George Heiron

Above. In 1950 the Western Region cast around for some new named trains - a ploy, it has been averred, to reintroduce chocolate and cream on some coaches.... The inaugural Red Dragon was on 5 June 1950, the up train running from Carmarthen to Swansea behind 7018 DRYSLLWYN CASTLE from Carmarthen to Swansea and thence to London with 5081 LOCKHEED HUDSON. Canton got Britannias from 1952 and the Pacifics could be seen on The Red Dragon from that year. The other WR Britannias were grouped at Cardiff later on, in 1956 and 1957 and one of them was FLYING DUTCHMAN, originally of Old Oak. In this quite exquisite photograph George Heiron caught it, beautifully etched in every detail, at Cardiff General in July 1958.

Below. Brand new Britannia No.70028 ROYAL STAR climbs the 1 in 300 through Chipping Sodbury in September 1952. It is sobering to recall the schedules of the such prestige trains as The Red Dragon; despite the stirring title its 1950 times were, by post-steam standards, pedestrian indeed. There were of course all sorts of problems, with fuel, labour and the permanent way after the war and the dearth which followed, but average speed was low, at a little under 50mph. It was double headed by Castles and Britannias on various occasions (*please* - have you photos out there?) and EVENING STAR even managed it for three days! Though we would all, doubtless, trade every HST ever invented for just one such trip behind a Castle or a Pacific, even at 48.5mph, it is a rum thought that, whilst the 1950 Red Dragon took 165 minutes, a HST in 1979 (they take a bit longer now, for nefarious reasons) did Newport - Swansea in 93 minutes.

Prior to the opening of the Severn Tunnel in 1886, the railway journey to South Wales was either circuitous or tedious. The circuitous route was via Gloucester, whereas the tedious route incorporated a ferry crossing between New Passage (near Pilning, on the east bank of the River Severn) and Portskewett (near Caldicot, on the west bank).

The railway, eleven and a half miles connecting Bristol and New Passage, was owned by the Bristol & South Wales Union Railway, but was worked by the GWR and, of necessity, laid with broad gauge rails. It opened to public traffic on 8 September 1863. At New Passage Pier there was a 271ft.-long platform on the Up side of the line; there was also a 319ft. platform entitled, somewhat confusingly, 'New Passage' just beyond the landward end of the pier, and this was used by all local passenger trains and two daily goods to and from Bristol. On the west side of the river, a spur of a little under one mile in length opened between the South Wales main line at Portskewett and the ferry pier on 1 January 1864.

The tides in the Severn Estuary are notorious, the difference between the high- and low-water marks at New Passage being as much as 50ft. - the second highest tidal range in the world - and an inevitable consequence is that the currents in the estuary are ferocious. The dangers of the tides were evidenced soon after the opening of the B&SWUR, an article in the February 1889 issue of the *GWR Magazine* including a story of a heavy gale from the south-west some months after the opening. The tide reached 4ft. 8in. above its proper level, and 'the waves raised by the gale were so large that they broke over the pier and the tops of the carriages standing upon it, and did much damage to the pier and the railway'. Nevertheless, dur-

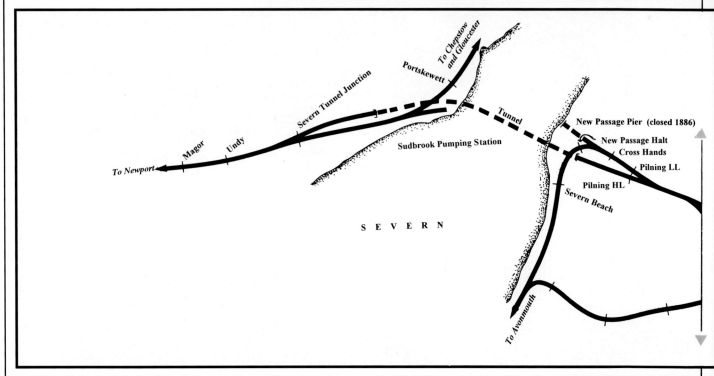

THROUGH THE HOLE

By Martin Smith

Fresh air at last...... Unless one is a former railwayman, it is difficult to imagine what footplate conditions were like during a trip through 'The Hole'. From the centre of the tunnel, there was a climb of 1 in 100 on the Gloucestershire side and 1 in 90 on the Monmouthshire side - the proverbial full head of steam, often from two locomotives, was absolutely essential. This magnificent picture shows an up goods emerging from the Gloucestershire side of the tunnel, with 3150 class 2-6-2T No.3159 piloting an unidentified 28XX 2-8-0. A number of the 3150s were allocated to Severn Tunnel Junction shed, principally for pilot and banking work through the tunnel - No.3159 was transferred to STJ in 1930, and remained there until withdrawn in 1949. It is believed that this picture was taken some time in the late 1920s or early 1930s. PHOTOGRAPH: G. SOOLE, COURTESY R.C. RILEY

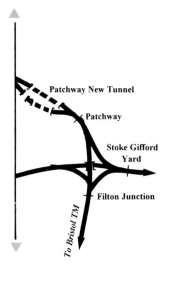

ing the life of the New Passage - Portskewett ferry there were no reports of serious accidents.

Inevitably, the Bristol & South Wales Union Railway was taken over by the GWR, but during its relatively short independent life, the B&SWUR had the customary entry in *Bradshaw's Shareholders' Guide*: *'....The (B&SWUR's) act also provides that the company may purchase an existing ferry across the Severn, called New Passage Ferry, and acquire and use steamboats for conveyance of passengers and goods..... By the Great Western Act, 1868, the Bristol and South Wales Un-* ion is merged into and amalgamated with the Great Western....'

The GWR clearly did not view the ferry crossing of the Severn as a long-term option, as plans for a railway tunnel under the Severn had been deposited as early as 1863. That scheme had been independently promoted, but had failed when its erstwhile supporters proved reluctant to stump up the cash; another representation two years later foundered for a similar reason. A completely different and ambitious scheme for a bridge across the estuary was later proposed, but that too came to nothing.

To the east of the Severn Tunnel, the main line negotiated Patchway Tunnel - or, to be precise, *tunnels*. There was originally only one to accommodate the single track through Patchway, but in 1887 a second line was built on a slightly different alignment, and this required a separate tunnel. On an unspecified date, probably late 1920s or early 1930s, an up parcels train heads east after having negotiated Patchway Tunnel. The down line is over the photographer's left shoulder, and can just be seen to the left of the signal box in the distance. The locomotives are 2-6-2T No.3176 and Bulldog 4-4-0 No.3392 NEW ZEALAND. PHOTOGRAPH: G. SOOLE, COURTESY R.C. RILEY

The idea for a tunnel under the Severn was revived by the GWR in 1872, the company obtaining an Act of Parliament in the name of the Severn Tunnel Railway for an eight mile line between Pilning and Rogiet, of which over half was to burrow under the river. To provide additional clout during the preliminaries, the GWR had asked the eminent engineer, Thomas Harrison, to give evidence in favour of the tunnel. Harrison was the North Eastern Railway's Chief Civil Engineer and, like many of his contemporaries, undertook consultancy work on a freelance basis, although his activities away from his home area are, these days, seldom remarked on.

As for the proposed Severn Tunnel, Harrison had been unconvinced that the river bed was not fissured and so he had declined to give the scheme his seal of approval. The GWR had then approached Sir John Hawkshaw, the designer of, amongst other things, Cannon Street and Charing Cross Bridges for the SER. Hawkshaw had been convinced of the soundness of the proposal, and later accepted the position of Consulting Engineer.

Prior to the commencement of the work, surveys paid particular attention to the main channel of the river, called The Shoots, which is some 300-400 yards wide and 80ft. deep at high-water. These surveys involved extensive and very precise depth soundings. Logically, it was decided

that the section under The Shoots would mark the centre point of the tunnel, the rail level being 50ft. below the rock bed and the bore rising on a gradient of 1 in 100 from each side.

Hawkshaw was fully aware of the tidal conditions in the Severn Estuary. Although the tunnel mouths were to be some distance from the river banks, the flatness of the land was such that every possible precaution had to be taken against flood water entering the mouths. Consequently, Hawkshaw demanded that the 'sea banks' around the tunnel mouth cuttings be built up to heights of 20ft. Despite the tidal conditions in the Severn Estuary, many locals considered that such precautions were laughably over-done, but Hawkshaw's research had revealed reports of the great floods of 1606 and 1702 and he was well aware of nature's ability to play tricks.

The preliminary work on the Severn Tunnel was undertaken by the GWR's own labour force, and started in March 1873. The first major step was to sink a shaft at Sudbrook (on the west bank) from which a 15ft.-diameter heading could be driven under the river. Work progressed rather slowly and, by August 1877, all that had been achieved was the sinking and lining of the shaft (later known as Old Shaft), the driving of some 1,600 yards of a 7ft.-square heading under the river, and the partial completion of a second (unlined) shaft in which it was

intended to fix the permanent pumps to drain the tunnel.

The GWR then decided to advertise for tenders for the whole work, but the three applications received were all rejected. Instead, it was decided to let two smaller contracts. One went to Oliver Norris of New Passage and was for the sinking of a shaft on the Gloucestershire side (later referred to as the Sea Wall Shaft), from which headings would be driven east and west. The other contract was awarded to Rowland Brotherhead of Chippenham, and entailed the sinking of two shafts (Marsh Shaft and Hill Shaft) to the west of Sudbrook, on the Monmouthshire side, and the driving of headings each way from them.

The work then progressed steadily but, in view of the vastness of the project, it was almost inevitable that mishaps would occur. The most serious happened on 16 October 1879, by which time the original heading from the Old Shaft had been driven eastwards for nearly two miles under the river and had reached to within 130 yards of the westward heading from Sea Wall Shaft. In Old Shaft, a large freshwater spring was suddenly struck, and water rushed in at the rate of 6,000 gallons per minute. Since another 2,400 gallons a minute were coming from the river heading, the pumps were eventually overpowered after operating for almost 24 hours at full speed. Fortunately, the men working in the heading were able to escape by means of a cross-heading into another shaft, but the works in the Old Shaft were flooded to the level of the river. It was a demoralising blow.

After reviewing the situation, the GWR appointed Hawkshaw to take full responsibility for the renewal of the work and, in December 1879 the experienced contractor, Thomas Walker, was hired to complete the entire undertaking, his contract being worth £948,959. Walker's description of his inheritance appears in MacDermot & Clinker's *History of the Great Western Railway*: 'Nothing could be more desolate than the appearance of the works at this time. There were near the main shaft only six cottages and a small office, the necessary boiler-houses and engine-houses, a small carpenter's shop, a fitter's shop, a blacksmith's shop, and two low buildings or sheds, used as cottages also. The tramway, which had been originally laid to Portskewett Station, had been pulled up, and in lieu of it another tramway had been laid, following (on the surface of the ground) the centre line of the tunnel itself from the Old Shaft to the Marsh Pit, and joining the Great Western Railway a mile west of Portskewett Station at Caldicot Pyll. The engines of the main shaft stood idle, the boilers were out of steam, most of the men who had been employed had left in search of other work, and the water in the shaft was standing up to the level of the high water in the Severn.

'The pumping engines at Sea Wall, Marsh, and High Pits were still at work,

as the working of those pits had been in the hands of Mr Norris and Mr Brotherhood; but no work was being done below, orders having been given to these gentlemen to suspend their operations.

'The pumps were able to keep the Hill Pit dry, but were not sufficiently powerful to drain either of the dipping headings from the Marsh or Sea Wall Shafts, while the main shaft and heading were full of water'.

Before work could recommence, it was essential to shut off the flood door in the long heading under the river. A plucky diver by the name of Lambert was given the dubious privilege of groping his way along the unfamiliar shaft in total darkness, with the added hazard of negotiating the debris left by the flood. When Lambert was within 70 yards of his target, he found that he could no longer drag his airpipe against the current of water and, therefore, decided to head back. On the return trip his airpipe became entangled in the beams and timbers of the heading but, in a feat of heroism worthy of *Boys' Own*, somehow managed to return to base safely.

The second stage in the story, complete with fashion notes for the sartorially-minded diver of the day, was described by Charles Richardson (Hawkshaw's right-hand man) in the January 1889 issue of the *GWR Magazine*: 'He (Lambert) was dreadfully disappointed at his failure; but the Contractor, having heard of the new apparatus

for diving without air pipes, which Fleuss, its inventor, was exhibiting daily at the London Aquarium, invited him to come down with his patent apparatus, and close the door.

'Fleuss accordingly came there, and went down with Lambert to the mouth of the heading; but when he (Fleuss) had groped about and found the sort of place he was expected to go into for nearly a quarter of a mile, his heart failed him and he came up again. He said that he would not undertake to go and close the door for ten thousand pounds.

'Lambert then asked him to lend him the dress and he (Lambert) would go; but this Fleuss refused to do. Then, however, the Contractor pointed out to him that he was standing in his own light, for if Lambert accomplished the job by the help of his (Fleuss's) patent dress it would be the best possible advertisement for him.

'Then Fleuss did consent. So, the next day, Lambert put on the dress and went down; but he failed in his first attempt, because the helmet he had to wear pinched his nose so tightly under the water pressure, that it brought on a terrible head-ache and he turned back again to have it altered.

'It must be explained that in this apparatus the breath has to be taken in through the nose and breathed out through the mouth, therefore, the nose pipe has to fit very tightly to the nose, and as Lambert's nose was very broad while Fleuss's was very thin, the nose pipe pinched him dreadfully, and he had

Just to the east of Patchway Tunnel, probably late 1920s or early 1930s (but definitely sometime between 1926 and 1935!), with 42XX 2-8-0T No.5255 on an up goods. There is clearly banking assistance at the rear. Note the separate down line on the left. PHOTOGRAPH: G. SOOLE, COURTESY R.C. RILEY

Having negotiated the Severn and Patchway Tunnels, an eastbound passenger train approaches Patchway station. The engine is 43XX 2-6-0 No.6369, and the train is formed of LNER stock. Everything points to this being the 'Ports-to-Ports Express' (Newcastle-Swansea) which was formed on alternate days of LNER and GWR stock - the engine too, supports this theory, for during the early 1930s it was allocated to Banbury, which provided the motive power for the Banbury-Swansea leg of the journey. But there is a fly in the ointment - prior to 1946 the 'Ports-to-Ports' was routed via Cheltenham, Gloucester and Chepstow, and not via the Swindon - Patchway - Severn Tunnel route. Could this have been a diverted working? PHOTOGRAPH: G. SOOLE, COURTESY R.C. RILEY

to get it altered. After this had been done, he went down again and succeeded in shutting the door'.

After Messrs. Lambert and Fleuss had resolved the problems with their dress, Sir John Hawkshaw decided that the tunnel should be lowered under The Shoots and along the Gloucestershire side by 15ft. This necessitated an increase in the gradient to 1 in 90 on the Monmouthshire side, in order to retain the original tunnel mouth.

Work on the tunnel was finally underway again in December 1880, but partial flooding occurred the following April. Nevertheless, the two headings were joined on 26 September 1881. Much work remained to be done, but when it looked as if the proverbial light was in sight, there were two major setbacks in quick succession. On 10 October 1883 the Great Spring broke once again, this time with even greater force than before. Seven days later a tidal wave flooded the low-lying land on the Monmouthshire side and poured into one of the tunnel shafts, Hawkshaw's high sea defences preventing even worse damage than would otherwise have occurred.

Our hero, Mr Lambert with the broad nose, was recalled to the scene to close the flood doors. With greater pumping power available, the works were subsequently cleared of water in less than a month. As a long-term solution to the problem of the Great Spring, Hawkshaw ordered that a new side heading be driven, parallel with

the line of the main tunnel. Six large Cornish beam engines were subsequently installed at Sudbrook for pumping, each capable of raising 5,000,000 gallons per day. The last three remained in use until November 1961, when they were replaced by electric pumps. By way of a footnote, in July 1901 the GWR renamed Achilles class 4-2-2 No.3055 LAMBERT, and at the time many enthusiasts assumed that the locomotive had been named in honour of the diver. The truth of the matter was, however, a little less exciting, as the engine had been named after the GWR General Manager, Henry Lambert, who had retired in 1896.

Early in 1884 Hawkshaw decided to reduce the length of the Severn Tunnel from 7,942 to 7,666 yards, by lengthening the approach cutting at the Monmouthshire end by 276 yards. The material extracted for the extension of the cutting was used in connection with siding accommodation at the new station near Rogiet - afterwards named Severn Tunnel Junction - which was effectively at the point where the Severn Tunnel line met the original South Wales main line (via Gloucester and Chepstow). The cutting on the Monmouthshire side was made through sandstone and so a steep-sided cutting was deemed perfectly safe, but the alluvial nature of the Gloucestershire bank dictated a cutting with more gently sloping banks, to prevent the risk of earth slips. Some 800,000 cubic yards had

to be excavated for the approach cutting on the Gloucestershire side and so, much to the entertainment of onlookers, the contractor used a new-fangled 'steam navvy'. This device was described at the time as having: 'the appearance of a gigantic spoon worked by a steam engine on wheels, and all under the control of one man who fills waggon after waggon with two spoon-fulls apiece'.

The brickwork for the tunnel was completed in April 1885, consuming some 76,400,000 bricks, which had been required to match the quality of Cattybrook or Staffordshire brindle bricks. The former type was made near Patchway (a few miles from the eastern end of the tunnel) whereas the latter was a great favourite of the GWR. The brick lining inside the tunnel was 27in. thick and the space between brickwork and the river bed was meticulously back-filled. Such specifications were necessary as the tunnel walls had to withstand a water pressure of 60lb psi, even with the provision of inverts.

The labour force engaged on building the tunnel and its approaches peaked at 3,628 men in 1884. To accommodate the men, streets of houses were built on both sides of the river, the purpose-built community at Sudbrook having hospitals, a chapel, and schools for the men's children. However, the contractor could not get the use of any land on the Gloucestershire side, and so the houses had to be built over the tunnel itself - on railway company property. Because the ground under the houses was likely to settle, they were built of timber, albeit with the fire precaution of heavy brick-built double chimneys between every second house. The ground moved significantly on one occasion, and although one chimney plummeted through the floor and out of sight, the wooden buildings were relatively unscathed. The only casualty was one man who, fearing an earthquake, jumped from a window and sprained his ankle. Nevertheless, there were many claims regarding waistcoats and trousers, containing money and valuables, which had been hung on nails driven into the vanished chimney.

The tunnel was virtually completed by the start of 1886 and, on 9 January, an Aberdare - Southampton coal train passed through it. The opening for regular traffic was delayed until the new pumping engines (mentioned earlier) and a gigantic 40ft.-diameter ventilation fan had been installed. The first scheduled goods trains passed through on 1 September and, after receiving the all-clear from the Board of Trade, Bristol - Cardiff passenger trains were routed through the tunnel as from 1 December.

The construction of Britain's longest railway tunnel (apart from those built later for underground lines in London) had taken 13 years, the final bill for the tunnel and its approaches being £1,806,248. Although Sir John Hawkshaw and Charles Richardson had described the Severn

Tunnel as being 7,666 yards (4m 626yd.) in length, the official figure was invariably given as 4m 628yd. The rails inside the tunnel were, incidentally, 68lb/yd and laid on longitudinal timbers, those on the approaches being 86lb/yd and laid on cross-sleepers.

The Severn Tunnel provided the GWR with a little sideline, one example of which was reported at the Locomotive, Carriage and Stores Committee meeting of 9 August 1905: *'The Locomotive Superintendent reported that he had acceded to an application received from Mr.C. Rymer for a supply of water, from this Co's Severn Tunnel main, to his cattle troughs at Caldicott [sic] upon payment of 4d per 1,000 gallons, £1 per annum meter rent and the cost of making the connection.... Approved'.*

Over the years, many similar arrangements were made for the use of the GWR's 'unwanted' water.

The line through the tunnel was built to the standard gauge, the old Bristol & South Wales Union line between Bristol and New Passage having been converted in August 1873. The ferry service between New Passage and Portskewett was discontinued as soon as the tunnel was opened for passenger traffic. The railway approaches to both ferry piers were closed, but part of the approach to Old Passage pier was eventually revived, more of which later. On the west bank of the Severn, Portskewett Pier had been destroyed by fire on 23 May 1881, and until temporary repairs to the pier had been completed on 15 June, Bristol - Cardiff trains had been routed via the re-

cently-opened Severn Bridge between Sharpness and Lydney. The bridge was owned by the independent Severn & Wye Railway which, at the time, had a far closer allegiance to the Midland Railway than the GWR.

It was, of course, anticipated that the Severn Tunnel route would become intensively used by coal trains from South Wales, as well as the Bristol - South Wales passenger services and other freight workings. Consequently, work was put in hand to double the line on the Bristol side of the tunnel. Doubling of the section between Narroways Hill (at St.Werburgh's in Bristol) and Patchway was completed on 27 May 1887. The Patchway - Pilning section was not ready until 27 May 1887, a new Up line having been built on a slightly different alignment - it was on a uniform gradient of 1 in 100 (instead of the 1 in 68 maximum of the existing Down line) and required the boring of a new tunnel, exactly one mile long, at the Patchway end, the old line passing through two tunnels, one of 1,246 yards and the other 62 yards.

Apart from the wholesale upgrading of the Bristol-Patchway section, the exit route for South Wales coal was further improved by the provision of a new loop between Dr Day's Junction and North Somerset Junction in Bristol, permitting direct running between the South Wales line and the directions of Bath, London and Southampton. During World War I the South Wales - South Coast route was one of several which gained consid-

No.3176 provides banking assistance for a heavy eastbound goods. The train is passing through Patchway station, having cleared the Severn and Patchway Tunnels, and the difficult climbs are now at an end. PHOTOGRAPH: G. SOOLE, COURTESY R.C. RILEY

A down express, hauled by what seems to be a Saint class 4-6-0, emerges from the Monmouthshire end of the Severn Tunnel. The line between Severn Tunnel Junction and Chepstow passes under the roadbridge on the right. The period is probably the 1920s.

erable strategic importance as an artery for bunker fuel, for warships. Figures quoted by MacDermot and Clinker reveal that, between 1913 and 1917, the number of trains (passenger and freight) passing through the tunnel each year rose from 18,099 to 24,027.

Communications on the Gloucestershire side were improved even more on 1 May 1903 when the new 'cut-off' route between Patchway and Swindon via Badminton and Wootton Bassett was opened throughout, passenger traffic via the new line commencing on 1 July. A substantial marshalling yard was established at Stoke Gifford, although the yard was primarily intended to handle traffic to and from Avonmouth Docks, which were treated to a direct rail connection to Stoke Gifford on 9 May 1910. The WTT for July-Sept 1910 states that the Stoke Gifford shunting engine was: 'To leave Loco Yard at 5.0am (MO 5.15am for Stoke Gifford and work 9.0am Stoke Gifford to Filton and back, and 11.50am Stoke Gifford to Pilning and back, shunt at Stoke Gifford and work traffic or run light Stoke Gifford to Bristol upon completion of work'. Stoke Gifford Yard ultimately had 14 roads in the Up yard and 10 in the Down, and remained in use until 1971, when part of the site was used for the construction of Bristol Parkway station.

To generations of railwaymen, the Severn Tunnel was known as 'The Hole'. A rather 'frontier spirit' account of a journey through the tunnel appeared in the July 1897 issue of *The Railway Magazine* - the writer of the article, Herbert Russell, had arranged a footplate ride on a Newport - London express, hauled by 4-2-2 No.3006 COURIER in order to provide yet another scoop:

'We were now close upon the black aperture, tearing down the incline which led to it at headlong speed. Evans [the driver] *blew a prolonged blast of the whistle, and while the resonant shriek swelled into many shrill and wild echoes from the high banks we plunged into the gloom, and in a breath, the daylight was eclipsed. The effect in the tunnel was strange, weird and impressive. The darkness seemed full of flying shadows; the ruddy gleams falling slantwise through the chinks betwixt the furnace doors, and the feeble glimmer of the lamp in the cab, tinged the piles of coal heaped up in the tender with blood-red hues. The figures of the driver and fireman showed in vague, shadowy shapes. Not the faintest glimmer came from the train in our wake; occasionally a little galaxy of sparks would vomit forth from the invisible chimney, and sweep like a flight of fireflies into the blackness behind. At intervals we flashed past lamps affixed to the damp walls, and once we passed a little band of men working by torchlight, and showing like demons in the*

A splendid photograph of an eastbound express emerging from the Severn Tunnel. We seem to be looking at a Saint class 4-6-0, mid- or late-1920s. Unfortunately, the alignment of the Pilning (Low Level)-Avonmouth line virtually above the tunnel entrance cannot be discerned.

The north side of Severn Tunnel Junction shed, 11 April 1944 - photograph taken from the coal stage embankment. It is possible that this picture was a 'before' shot, taken as a record of the scene prior to construction of the new repair shop.

wavering glare. Somewhere about the middle of the tunnel another train passed us, spinning by in a long undulating streak of light, with pale clouds of steam dimly visible. The roar and rattle raised by our passage was deafening, yet shrill above it all rose the reverberant scream of the whistle, which the driver continually blew.'

There is much else in similar vein, in the wonderfully melodramatic tone which so characterises prose of the time. Among the many other recorded tales of working through the Severn Tunnel there are several instances of 'what might have been',

including the occasion when, on 23 June 1943, Hall 4-6-0 No.6937 (not then named) was running light towards South Wales and passed a danger signal at Severn Tunnel East. The engine continued its journey through the tunnel, and was only stopped by a flag signalman near Severn Tunnel West box.

In his book *Great Western Saints and Sinners*, W.A. Tuplin relates a story believed to be based on the exploits of Star 4-6-0 No.4044 PRINCE GEORGE which, on 6 December 1946, was at the head of the 5.35pm Portsmouth - Cardiff passenger working.

Tuplin tells how the driver and fireman were momentarily distracted by some minor crisis on the footplate and, when their concentration was restored, neither man could recall having seen a signal which they had been anticipating. With safety in mind, they decided to stop the engine, the fireman subsequently being volunteered to walk back through the tunnel and, with the aid of a hand-lamp, see if the signal had indeed been passed. After the fireman had been gone for what seemed to be a very long time, the driver decided he should walk forward from the engine to see if the signal was actually ahead. This was all very laudable, but for a couple of oversights. Neither the driver nor the fireman had fully closed the small injector, nor had the tender handbrake been fully applied. The first inkling the driver had of these mental aberrations was when he heard his crew-less train approaching from behind.

The story goes that the locomotive and train continued down the gradient and part of the way up the slope on the other side, then rolled back down the gradient almost to its original spot, forward once more, then back again - the locomotive and train seesawing over the bottom level of the tunnel no less than four times before the driver managed to scramble aboard and bring it to a halt. Tuplin tells how the driver waited for his fireman to rejoin the train, and then resumed the journey with both men mentally scribbling plausible cover stories. The tale is amusingly told but, with all due respect to Tuplin, it has been suggested that the events of the day were not *quite* so momentous.

Back to the nitty-gritty. Maintenance of the Severn Tunnel was the responsibility of the Divisional Engi-

Severn Tunnel Junction shed, looking east, 11 April 1944 - photograph taken from the top of the water softener. The right-hand double track bay of the shed building was a 'Loans Act' addition - built with money made available under its terms of 1929. Note the new ash shelter on the extreme left of the frame - this was wartime, and the shelter (designed to eliminate the glow from red hot ash being dropped at night) was also camouflaged. The main lines are on the right, the farthest being the Chepstow and Gloucester lines, and to their immediate left the lines to the Severn Tunnel descend gradually. In the distance on the left is the village of Rogiet.

neer at Bristol, under the general supervision of the Chief Engineer. The inspection and maintenance of the track was carried out by a permanent way inspector whose headquarters were at Stapleton Road station in Bristol. The duties of the PW inspector included walking through the tunnel at least once each week, and frequently riding through on a locomotive. For many years the daily maintenance of the track in the tunnel required the attentions of 24 men; they were divided into three gangs, each comprising a ganger, a sub-ganger and six men. Each gang was responsible for a section of a mile and a half.

The problem of illumination for the gangs working in the tunnel was discussed in the *GWR Magazine* of May 1938: '....*from time to time electric and oil-pressure lamps have been tested. We have at present many oil-pressure lamps in use in tunnels, but have not entirely withdrawn the open flame type in long tunnels. Firstly, the electric and oil-pressure lamps are both liable from many reasons to sudden failure, which would produce a condition of extreme discomfort and danger, whereas the naked flame type can only fail from lack of oil, of which they give fair warning, and to cope with which stocks of oil are kept in the tunnels. And secondly, a vital point is that the approach of trains is immediately known to the men by the movement of the flame, and an efficient substitute for this warning has still to be found'*.

At the time that piece was written the GWR had recently introduced its streamlined diesel railcars, and it was appreciated that the comparatively stealthy approach of a railcar could pose a safety hazard for the tunnel gangs. The solution was to equip the gangers and look-outs with watches which had been synchronised at the start of the day with the signalmen's clocks. The gangers were under orders to stand clear five minutes before the scheduled passage of each diesel car and the signalmen either end instructed not to permit the cars to enter the tunnel before the prescribed times. During the late 1930s the gangs worked in the tunnel between 8.30am and 4.30pm on weekdays and from 8.30am to 12.10pm on Saturdays (a 42-hour week), and during a weekday shift the average number of trains scheduled to pass through the tunnel was sixty, of which four were diesel cars.

An interesting point which has been raised is that, in the days of single driver steam locomotives, the absence of coupling rods also resulted in a relatively quiet approach, and several fatal accidents elsewhere were blamed on the victims not hearing approaching engines. The necessity for extreme vigilance by gangs working in the Severn Tunnel was not exclusive to the diesel era.

The Severn Tunnel originally formed one block section, but intermediate signalling was introduced in 1942. *The Railway Magazine* described the arrangements in 1942 - the tunnel clearances made it impossible to protect against breakaways it was explained, and sufficient distance had to be available beyond any stop signal on the falling gradient, allowing a train to gain impetus for the subsequent ascent. The intermediate signals were thus placed one mile from the entrances and to ensure that poor visibility constituted no danger, the intermediate signals were duplicated by repeater signals, and automatic train control used.... '....*The control circuits ensure an indication that all signal-lamps are burning correctly. The starting-signal lever is front-locked electrically, and proves the track-circuit sections unoccupied to the overlap point. The front-lock circuit of the intermediate signal lever proves "line clear" received on the block, and the overlap track-circuit unoccupied. The pulling of the lever necessitates a second "line clear" signal before the front-lock can be freed again. The back-lock is freed provided the red and yellow lights become illuminated correctly in the intermediate signal and its repeater signal'*.

The new signalling arrangements were, however, not a great success. The track circuiting in the tunnel was badly affected by the damp conditions, and engine crews were not over enthusiastic about an unnecessary stop in the middle of the tunnel, for it meant a standing start for the uphill climb to the daylight.

Another change in operations came during World War II, in that the use of special brake vans was discontinued. Prior to 1942/43 special Severn Tunnel brake vans manned by 'experienced guards' had been added to heavy freight trains passing through, the idea being to provide additional braking on the downhill gradients and to keep the couplings taut, thereby reducing the risk of breakaways. The special brake vans were enclosed (as a safeguard against the poisonous sulphur fumes), and the general practice was for a van to be run up an inclined siding to await its train. When the train stopped, the van ran down the siding by gravity to be attached to the train. The lack of 'experienced guards' during the war years forced the special vans out of use.

****

As mentioned earlier, part of the defunct Pilning - New Passage section of the old Bristol & South Wales Union line was later resuscitated. On 5 February 1900 the Avonmouth & Severn Tunnel Railway (a thinly disguised subsidiary of the GWR) opened seven and three quarters of a mile of single track line between Pilning Junction and Avonmouth, the first mile and three quarters westwards from Pilning using the alignment of the old New Passage line. According to Mike Vincent, the author of *Lines to Avonmouth*, the rails on the remaining section of the B&SWU (between the Avonmouth line and New Passage) were not lifted until 11 March 1917, over thirty years after they had been last used. The new Pilning - Avonmouth line was intended to handle only freight traffic, but a regular passenger service was introduced on 9 July 1928 and the name New Passage revived for a halt which was established almost at the point where the 'new' Avonmouth line diverged from the deceased New Passage line. A new halt was also provided at Cross Hands, quarter of a mile east of New Passage. The Pilning - Avonmouth line of 1900 was built on a similar alignment to that of a line proposed by the B&SWU almost 40 years earlier.

At Pilning, a single platform on the Avonmouth line - on the site of the original B&SWU platform - was opened for the commencement of passenger services in 1928. It took the name Pilning (Low Level), the existing station on the Severn Tunnel line becoming 'High Level'. In common with the halts at New Passage and Cross Hands, its platform was only 150ft. long and could therefore accommodate only two carriages; lengthier trains often appeared on the line, but passengers wishing to alight at any of the three halts had to ensure that they were travelling in the appropriate carriages. A nice example of typical country branch practices is given in *Lines to Avonmouth*, the author explaining that the responsibility for trimming and lighting the gas lamps at New Passage and Cross Hands halts was in the care of the station masters at Severn Beach and Pilning respectively. The guard of the last train each day was charged with extinguishing the lights, collecting them, and returning them to the duty signalman at Pilning.

During World War I it had been intended to lay new sidings and rebuild the signal box on the low level line at Pilning, but although a new 'box was provided (at Government expense) the idea for the sidings was dropped. Similarly, a proposal to double the line between Pilning Junction and Hallen Marsh Junction (on the Avonmouth line) was abandoned. Passenger services were withdrawn from the Pilning (LL) to Severn Beach section of the Avonmouth line on 23 November 1964, DMUs having monopolised during the final years. With the closure of the Low Level station at Pilning the main line High Level station lost its suffix, and reverted to plain old Pilning on 6 May 1968.

In 1924 facilities were provided for the conveyance of motor cars through the Severn Tunnel. Prior to this initiative, motorists wishing the cross the Severn had had a choice either of the precarious looking ferry from Aust to Beachley or the very circuitous route via Gloucester. The GWR provided special carriage trucks, on which cars could be loaded, and kept them on permanent standby at Severn Tunnel Junction, Pilning and Patchway. The company stipulated

Sudbrook pumping house, 11 July 1959. The rail connection was by means of a spur from the Severn Tunnel Junction - Chepstow line. PHOTOGRAPH: R.M. CASSERLEY

that 24 hours' notice was required to use the trucks but, perhaps predictably, this was of little use to non-locals who, unfamiliar with train timings, turned up on chance. Nevertheless, the car trucks remained a feature of the local stations until the opening of the road bridge across the Severn in 1966. Some say that if they were still available today, they might often be quicker than a bridge crossing....

The GWR Traffic Committee minutes of 27 March 1924 reported on the: *'Extension of down loop and refuge siding (at Pilning) and provision of "scissors" crossing'*, the total cost of £2,412 being divided among the Engineering

Department (£1,437), Signal Engineer (£525) and Chief Mechanical Engineer (£450). In the absence of further information, perhaps it can be assumed that that work was in preparation for the use of the car trucks. As an aside, the same minutes included a reference to: *'Pilning: Erection of houses for Station Master and Inspector ....£1,400'.*

The availability of the car trucks and the stipulations regarding the use thereof found a way into the public timetables. The WR public timetables for summer 1955, for

example, listed the following weekday services *(as below)*.

There were also two services available every Sunday, with a third during the peak season.

The safety precautions for those using the car trucks were firmly laid down: *'A quantity of petrol (not exceeding one quart in the case of motor cycles) may be left in the tanks provided that:*

(a) in the case of vehicles with gravity or autovac feed, the flow of petrol to the carburettor has been stopped by means of the shut-off cock provided

(b) in the case of vehicles with electric petrol pump, the flow of petrol to the carburettor be interrupted by switching off the electric pump (switch key, if fitted, must be removed)

(c) with cars fitted with mechanical petrol pumps, the engine is stopped and the ignition key removed

(d) the motor is free from the leakage of petrol.'

Can anything like this be imagined now? The fares for single journeys were listed as 13s/4d for cars up to 8hp and 16s/1d for those over 8hp - somewhat less than it costs to drive over the Severn Bridge these days. Tarpaulins were available for covering the car, for a fee of 2s/6d but, despite the filthy conditions in the tunnel, many motorists balked at the cost.

****

On the Monmouthshire side of the Severn, a corrugated iron twin road

	MO	SO		ES	SO		
Pilning HL dep.	8.20am	10.15am		10.25am	5.00pm	6.37pm	8.35pm
Sev. Tun. Jn arr.	8.33am	10.28am		10.38am	5.25pm	7.03pm	8.48pm
	SO		ES				
Sev. Tun. Jn dep	9.15am	9.26am		2.44pm	7.48pm		
Pilning HL arr.	9.27am	9.47am		3.00pm	8.02pm		

The interior of Sudbrook pumping house, 11 July 1959. A remarkable - but absolutely essential - appendage to the Severn Tunnel. PHOTOGRAPH: H.C. CASSERLEY

On board the 4.40pm car train at Severn Tunnel Junction station, 14 July 1958. Loading was actually undertaken in the bays *behind* the railings on the left - additional 'Carflat' trucks are standing in one of the bays. PHOTOGRAPH: R.M. CASSERLEY

of 56XX 0-6-2Ts, and ten assorted 0-6-0ST/PTs. The influx of 3150s had started in the late 1920s after displacement from other duties, and their new employment consisted mainly of piloting through 'The Hole'. Because of the conditions in the tunnel, the job of keeping them clean was often regarded as an impossible task. By the end of 1947 a total of 22 3150s was based at Severn Tunnel Junction, their duties by then including semi-fast passenger turns.

At the start of 1948, 93 locomotives were allocated to Severn Tunnel Junction. Apart from the 22 3150s and eight other 2-6-2Ts, the stud of tank engines comprised ten 72XX 2-8-2Ts, four 42XX 2-8-0Ts, eleven 0-6-2Ts (including two ex-Brecon & Merthyr locos), ten assorted 0-6-0PTs and one 517 class 0-4-2T. The tender engines consisted of five 4-6-0s (one Saint and four Granges), eighteen 2-8-0s (all 28XXs but for a WD), two 43XX 2-6-0s, and a pair of veteran Dean Goods 0-6-0s. The shed closed to steam in October 1965 and after a few years use by

engine shed was provided at Severn Tunnel Junction in December 1886. It was on the north side of the line at the eastern end of the station, and was equipped with a 45ft. 3in. diameter turntable. By the early 1900s the shed was in dire need of replacement, a Locomotive Committee minute of 20 December 1905 explaining that: *'Upon the representation of the Locomotive Superintendent it was agreed to recommend negotiations for the acquisition of 6 acres of land at Severn Tunnel Junction ....for the erection of an Engine Shed and the provision of a turntable at that place. The Locomotive Superintendent submitted a plan shewing how it is proposed to carry out the work at an estimated cost of £16,150. After consideration it was agreed to recommend the Board to sanction the expenditure'.*

A minute of 12 December 1906 noted that: *'Fencing of land in connection with the construction of a new Engine Shed: Additional expenditure £397.'*

The new four road Churchward-style double ended straight shed was brought into use (a little to the east of the station) in December 1907, although the original shed of 1886 was retained for use by railmotors until the mid-1920s. The site of the original shed, incidentally, was that on which the car dock was eventually built. The shed was extended by the addition of a twin road bay, the coal stage/turntable improved and an ash shelter provided under Ministry of War Transport direction in 1944, at a cost of over £35,000. The Repair Shop was born out of the same building episode. Under GWR auspices Severn Tunnel Junc-

tion shed was coded 'STJ', the more-familiar code of 86E being applied after Nationalisation.

Throughout its life, the shed's allocation consisted mainly of freight engines. The Swindon register for 1 January 1909 - when the shed was only around a year old - reveals a complement of 28 locomotives: sixteen assorted 0-6-0STs, five Aberdare 2-6-0s, three 2800 class 2-8-0s (including the first, No.97 as it then was), two 3150 class 2-6-2Ts, a Standard Goods 0-6-0 tender engine, and a Metro 2-4-0T. The shed's first brand-new 28XX, No.2802 incidentally, had been received on 18 October 1905.

By 1 January 1934, the allocation had grown to 57. These comprised: seven Aberdare 2-6-0s, ten 28XX and three ROD 2-8-0s, a Bulldog 4-4-0, three Dean Goods 0-6-0s, five 43XX Moguls, sixteen 3150 2-6-2Ts, a pair

diesels, the building was given over to a car distribution firm, until being demolished.

An important task for STJ engines was banking through the Severn Tunnel, the WTT for July-September 1910 listing 1 - 9 as above.

Although main line diesels had appeared on the Western Region in 1958, steam still predominated in

No	Mondays from	to	Tues-Fris from	to	Saturdays from	to	Sundays from	to	from	to
1	6.0am	4.0pm	11.30am	9.30pm	11.30am	9.30pm				
2	5.0pm	3.0am	6.30pm	4.30pm	7.0pm	5.0am				
3	8.0pm	6.0am	8.0pm	6.0am	8.30pm	6.30am				
4	8.30pm	6.30am	9.0pm	7.0am	9.30pm	7.30am				
5	10.30pm	8.30am	10.30pm	8.30am	11.55pm	9.55am				
6			12.5am	10.5am	12.5am	10.5am	1.0am	11.0am		
7			2.0am	12noon	2.0am	12noon	3.30am	1.30pm		
8	1.45pm	11.45pm	3.30am	1.30pm	3.30am	1.30pm				
9			6.0am	4.0pm	6.0am	4.0pm				

No	Starting time	Authorised hours from starting time							Total (week)
		M	T	W	Th	F	Sa	Su	
1	12.45am(*)	14½	14½	14½	14½	14½	14½	-	87
2	1.45am(*)	14½	14½	14½	14½	14½	14½	-	87
3	3.30am(*)	14½	14½	14½	14½	14½	14½	-	87
4	2.35am(MO)	7½	-	-	-	-	-	-	7½
5	6.00am	14½	14½	14½	14½	14½	14½	-	87
6	10.15am	13¾	14½	14½	14½	14½	14½	2¾	87
7	2.30pm	9½	14½	14½	14½	14½	14½	5	87
8	4.00pm	8	14½	14½	14½	14½	14½	6½	87
9	5.30pm	6½	14½	14½	14½	14½	14½	8	87
10	6.35pm	5¼	14½	14½	14½	14½	14½	9	87
11	8.30pm	3½	14½	14½	14½	14½	14½	11	87
12	7.00am(*)	7½	14½	14½	14½	14½	14½	-	80
13	10.00pm(#)	2	16	16	16	16	16	6	88

*Different starting times on Mondays. #Duty suspended

1960, as evidenced by the weekday *Banking Engine Roster* for Severn Tunnel Junction shed that year *(Bottom left page)*.

On Sundays four banking rosters were shown. These comprised one six and a half hour stint starting at 4.45pm, and three fourteen and a half hour turns, the first starting at 5.30pm, the second at 6.00pm and the third at 10.00pm. The point-to-point running times for assistant engines returning light were - Pilning-Severn Tunnel East:4 minutes; Severn Tunnel East-Severn Tunnel West: 8 minutes; Severn Tunnel West-Severn Tunnel Jctn: 3 minutes.

There was, of course, an extensive marshalling yard at Severn Tunnel Junction. Prior to 1931 it dealt with traffic between the Cardiff and Newport Districts and the South and West of England and London and also traffic from the Swansea District to the South and West of England. London District traffic from west of Bridgend was dealt with, not at Severn Tunnel Junction, but at Stoke Gifford Yard, several miles beyond the eastern end of the tunnel. In the late 1920s the GWR was quick to see the financial advantages of the 'Loans and Guarantees Act', a Government scheme intended to make moneys available for large engineering projects which could help to reduce unemployment, and one of the GWR's 'Loans Act' schemes was the modernisation of facilities at Severn Tunnel Junction.

The works involved extending the yard to increase capacity from 1,405 to 2,652 wagons, and this permitted the handling of West Wales - London traffic to be transferred from Stoke Gifford to Severn Tunnel Junction. As the main line at Severn Tunnel Junction was on an embankment, and because of the nature of the ground, it was not possible to concentrate the traffic in one new 'hump' yard, but the new arrangement nevertheless improved efficiency, with Up trains being received at one of three reception sidings. On the Down side of the line, the cost of building a double-ended yard was considered prohibitive, but the 19 sidings were divided into three groups so that three shunting engines could work simultaneously. The yard was provided with gas flood-lighting.

Moving ahead to 1960, the WTT for the summer of that year lists the general shunting rosters for Severn Tunnel Junction locomotives. They were *(as below)*.

* Shunting duty No 6 took in the Up Side and Mileage Yard, also mileage and cripple Sidings.

The same 1960 WTT included a table of maximum engine loadings through the Severn Tunnel for parcels, milk and fish trains: King, 500tons; BR Class 9 2-10-0, 455tons; County, Castle, BR Class 7, 455tons; Hall, Grange, BR Class 5, 420tons*; Manor, 43XX, 51XX, 61XX, 81XX, 56XX, BR Class 4, 406tons; 45XX, 57XX, BR Class 3, 336tons; 2251, BR Class 2, 308tons; 90XX, light 0-6-0T, 280tons; 14XX, 58XX 0-4-2T, 196tons.**

*Halls permitted 430tons for parcels, milk and fish

**Reduced to 170tons in eastbound direction.

A social history of Severn Tunnel Junction (written by W.C. Winter for the *Gwent Local History Journal*) lurks in the extensive archives of the Welsh Railways Research Circle. Mr Winter explains that three terraces of houses - Ifton Terrace, Rogiet Terrace and Sea View Terrace - were built by the GWR for its employees very shortly after the opening of Severn Tunnel Junction station. In the 1920s the Great Western Garden Village Society built additional staff housing, with financial aid forthcoming from the Treasury and Chepstow Rural District Council. During the inter-war years a hostel was built between the station and the engine shed, and was used as a 'lodge' by those engaged on double-home turns. During World War II fifty concrete prefabs were erected locally for railway staff; sleeping coaches were also provided, and these were kept in the car dock. The importance of Severn Tunnel Junction as a railway centre can be gauged from the fact that, at the start of the war, some 1,050 people were employed by the railway in various capacities.

A very local duty serviced by Severn Tunnel Junction shed was the working of the single track Sudbrook branch, which diverged from the Gloucester line about a mile and three quarters east of Severn Tunnel Junction station. The branch was actually laid almost on top of the tunnel, and was used primarily to take coal to the pumping engines at Sudbrook.

A secondary usage of the Sudbrook branch involved the movement of 'sludge tanks'. The water for Severn Tunnel Junction shed was pumped from the River Severn and, of necessity, was softened by chemical treatment. The resultant sludge was taken from the softening plant to Sudbrook in the 'sludge tanks' which were, in fact, old locomotive tenders. The working instructions for the Sudbrook branch stipulated that a maximum of three of these loaded

tanks were permitted in any single 'train'. In 1959 sidings were laid on the branch to serve a pulp mill, which used water pumped from the tunnel.

In 1944 a ground frame was installed to work the connection between the Sudbrook branch and the new Down goods loop. The working instructions for the branch were amended for the new method of operation, and also explained that: *'Any class of GW Engine (excluding only the 60XX King and 2-8-0 (H) 47XX) may be permitted to work over the Sudbrook Branch for a distance of 1,276 yards beyond the stop lamp at the commencement of the Branch. The limit is defined by a red engine stop post situated 25 yards from the level crossing known as "Post Office".*

'Any engine, as permitted above, may be used to push wagons into the Loop Siding at the "Five Mile Four" pumping station at both ends, but the engines themselves must not work beyond the clearing point in the Siding at either end'.

The mention in the above extract of "Five Mile Four" is a reference to the Sudbrook pumping shaft, located five miles four chains from the start of the Severn Tunnel line at Pilning Junction. Although all but two types of GWR engines were permitted on the Sudbrook branch in 1944, the 1960 WTT was somewhat less generous: *'22XX and 57XX Class Engines may work over the Branch subject to observance of service Restrictions'.*

Apart from the 'sludge tanks' and, after 1959, the occasional train of timber for the pulp mill, the Sudbrook branch appears to have been served by one train each day. This, it is assumed, brought in coal for the pumping engines and returned with the empties. Nowadays, the tunnel emergency train is stored in a secure compound at Sudbrook.

The Severn Tunnel is, of course, still in regular use today but, inevitably, present-day railway activities at either end of the tunnel are not what they used to be. These days, another railway tunnel is regularly grabbing the headlines and is hailed as a marvel of modern engineering. That 'other' tunnel may well warrant the praise, but it should never be forgotten that, almost 110 years ago, the Severn Tunnel was, at the time, as great an engineering achievement as that 'other' tunnel is today.

Contributor's note: Sincere thanks are due to Mr Bill Peto of the Great Western Society and to Mr Ray Caston of the Welsh Railways Research Circle for their invaluable advice and assistance during the preparation of this article.

No	Starting time	Authorised hours from starting time							Total		
		M	T	W	Th	F	Sa	Su	(week)	Work	
1	6.00am	18	24	24	24	24	24	6	144	Down Hump	
2	10pm(Su)	24	24	24	24	24	24	16	160	Down Yard	
3	6.00am	18	24	24	24	24	24	6	144	Down Yard	
4	6.00am	18	24	24	24	24	24	6	144	Bristol Yard	
5	6.00am	18	24	24	24	24	24	6	144	Up Hump	
6	2.00pm	8	8	8	8	8	8	-	48	*	

Above. West Country No.34051 WINSTON CHURCHILL brings in a heavy Waterloo - Plymouth express in June 1953. The girders indicate Fisherton Street - 'Fisherton' was the name of the station when built at the end of the 1850s, and the curve here is a relic of disagreements between the LSWR and the GWR - the exaggerated Salisbury curve was necessary to accommodate the Great Western's terminus, off to the left. The curious 'Market House Branch' dived off to the right, through the trees to the left of the 'W. Main & Son' building. PHOTOGRAPH George Heiron.

Above. Proving that brute power can be attractive. An early Heiron essay, a bit scratched and scruffed but a marvellous image. The locomotive is 35011 GENERAL STEAM NAVIGATION, backing on to an Exeter - Waterloo express, in June 1948. The building on the left is part of the surviving GWR terminus. PHOTOGRAPH George Herion.

Fourum

*Princessly Progress
in the 1950s*

Above. To some observers of West Coast affairs the Princess Pacifics could be something of an enigma. They were renowned indeed but south of Crewe a Princess was something of a *rara avis*. This is 46200 THE PRINCESS ROYAL on the up fast, coming south out of Northchurch Tunnel (north of Berkhamsted) in the 1950s.

Below. THE PRINCESS ROYAL again, tearing along through its unaccustomed terrain, the Home Counties, with *The Shamrock*. For much of their working lives the Princess Royals were divided between Edge Hill (five engines) and Crewe North (seven) and apart from two or three daily workings from Liverpool to London were more at home on trains to the north of their provincial retreats.

Above. South East stranger again. 46212 DUCHESS OF KENT pulls away from a signal check at Watford Junction with the up *Shamrock* in the 1950s. In these years the Princess Royal Pacifics played second fiddle to the Coronations but their demise was fairly protracted; the end began in 1961 with the ascendancy of the EE Type 4s and ended, through bouts of storage, cannibalisation and so on, in 1963.

Below. The Liverpool link again - 46208 PRINCESS HELENA VICTORIA with the up *Merseyside Express*. The Watford dc lines lie in the foreground.

UNITED STATES on her maiden voyage at the Ocean Terminal, 1952. Photograph Les Elsey.

SOMETHING ON

By D.W. Winkworth

Something on Southampton? appeared in the editor's bold hand writing at the bottom of the letter. First reaction to this was that it might be a tip for a gee-gee in a forthcoming race, or perhaps, a long shot at the next winners of the F.A. Cup but, on reflection, it dawned that it was a nudge for a typescript on some aspect of railway working in the Southampton area. Writing to order, especially if of a pot-boiling nature, is not the most attractive way of proceeding for this author so thoughts turned to how to produce something new and non-hackneyed for readers' enjoyment and, maybe, enlightenment.

Millbrook Graving Dock Platform

Southampton, of course, is docks, Docks and DOCKS and so the opportunity has been grasped to write about three very different dock stations which have not been the subjects of extended reference hitherto. First of these three, chronologically, is Millbrook Graving Dock Platform. The first thing to notice is the term *platform* which is not typical of Southern Railway practice, being more usually the preserve of that line to the north - the Great Western Railway. However, the SR invested its Docks and Marine department at Southampton with a degree of autonomy in its day to day operation and that is doubtless how the terminology originated. A temporary passenger platform had been built

within the docks at the time of the 1911 Naval Review and perhaps it was natural to perpetuate the description for another such within the docks purlieu.

Both the London & South Western Railway and particularly its successor, the Southern Railway, had made great efforts to improve and expand facilities at Southampton Docks and in 1924 a new floating dry dock had been brought into commission. It transpired, however, that even this new dock would not be able to accommodate either of the two new ocean liners proposed by the Cunard Steamship Company for the North Atlantic shuttle service. So, the SR decided to incorporate in its new docks extension a graving dock of adequate size to service the 'No.534', then building at Clydebank, later to be known as the QUEEN MARY. In the event, there were funding difficulties and the dock became ready before the ship. A royal opening was arranged with the royal yacht steaming into the dock. After disembarking, H.M. The King would declare the dock open and his consort name it King George V Graving Dock. After the ceremony the party would re-embark and sail away, the duty performed.

The day fixed was 26th July 1933. Stands were erected at the head of the dock with access over a footbridge from Church Lane, Millbrook. While this might prove satisfactory for

the school children and lesser lights on the guest list it clearly was not suitable for the main body of invitees, many of whom would be arriving by special train from Waterloo or elsewhere. Millbrook station's location did not lend itself to easy reception of guests, especially as an area to the west was to become a temporary car park for the event. Accordingly, a temporary loop line from the down line at the west end of Millbrook station was installed, rejoining the down line at Church Lane footbridge. To the south of this loop was constructed a platform, 656 feet long, for use by passengers of the special trains, to be known as Millbrook Graving Dock Platform.

Meticulous arrangements were made for the occasion, including the loan of RMS BERENGARIA by Cunard to the SR so that luncheon could be taken on board after the ceremonial opening of the new dock in the morning. The special notice issued by the Traffic Controller, Southampton, indicated that a 'Special Train with distinguished guests will leave No.44 shed' (old docks where the BERENGARIA was berthed) 'at 10.30am sharp for Millbrook Graving Dock platform' and would return at 1.15pm due at No.44 shed at 1.30pm. Additionally there was an empty train from the Millbrook platform - presumably having come from Waterloo - which was due at the Old Docks Gate at 11.30am and was to form the 4.20pm guest special from No.44 shed to London (Waterloo). The best laid plans of mice and men sometimes go adrift, nonetheless.

At 7.25am on the morning of the event the driver of the 6.40am Southampton Terminus to Waterloo via Alton train overran the signal at Winchester Junction and derailed his engine and tender on the points as the signalman was setting the line for the branch. For this driver Toop was rewarded with a year's shunting duties, to allow him to reflect on his misdemeanour. Fortunately, although the up line was blocked, necessitating diversions via Andover, it was possible to pass traffic under caution on the down line after 9.27am so that, presumably, the down special from London to Millbrook was able to pass. The up line was cleared at 2.36pm so no delay would be occasioned to the return special to Waterloo.

With this unexpected hurdle surmounted and the royal ceremony successfully completed, the general manager and directors were entitled to relax en route from Millbrook to No.44 shed and lunch. However, to general dismay and contrary to instructions laid down, the train came to a halt at Empress Yard, where the yard foreman insisted that the main line engine be detached from the train and a dock departmental engine conclude the journey to shed No.44. As a consequence the foreman was suspended from duty and a local enquiry followed within a day or so at which he was severely reprimanded but allowed to resume duty as a foreman. This was not very well received when reported to Waterloo and the Docks and Marine Manager had to stomach a rebuke by letter from the Assistant General Manager. This included such remarks as *'I question whether a man who takes the action that Foreman X did on the 26th July is suited to be a Foreman. However, I presume you have acquainted him of the displeasure of the General Manager ...'* Such were the events associated with the one-day life of Millbrook Graving Dock Platform. It truly was A Day in the Life...

The Ocean Terminal
Eventually, the QUEEN MARY came into service and later, during the war, her sister ship QUEEN ELIZABETH. The Cunard White Star Company (as it had become in 1934) did not favour the berths in the new docks, and continued using the Ocean Dock in the old docks. During the war the shed (No.44) serving this berth had been damaged by enemy air action and after hostilities ended the two ships concluded their trooping careers and were handed back for refitting. The Southern Railway had dutifully named one of its Merchant Navy class engines after the steamship line, Pullman cars were being renovated for the connecting train service to and from London Waterloo but the weak link was the bomb-damaged customs shed in which draughty waits were to be made by passengers, who were otherwise cosseted throughout.

The then Docks and Marine manager, R.P. Biddle, was well aware of the situation and wrote on 21st November 1945 to Sir Eustace Missenden, the general manager, asking for permission to proceed with plans for the complete rebuilding of shed No.44, in order to offer modern

SOUTHAMPTON

Glorious *art deco* 'ship's bridge' effect of the Ocean Terminal, seaward end, September 1953. Photograph Les Elsey.

facilities to passengers. Various discussions followed from this and Biddle developed his ideas. In company with a staff architect, he undertook a visit to North America and Canada where installations at New York, Philadelphia, Baltimore, Washington, Boston, Chicago, Montreal and Halifax were studied. On 15th April 1946 he submitted a long report on this visit indicating that the SR had little to learn from operations in those two countries and, with its new Ocean Terminal, would lead the world.

Just over a month later Biddle sent detailed proposals, complete with drawings and estimates of cost, to the general manager. Biddle advocated sweeping away the bomb-damaged 34 year old sheds and constructing a new two-storey building of which the upper floor would have waiting rooms, buffets, information, postal and ticket kiosks and customs accommodation leaving the lower floor free for use as a railway station, a circulating area for cars and road traffic and a cargo area. Two boat trains, each of 14 coaches, would be dealt with at an island platform with one face for a Pullman train and the other for a train for the secondary class (instead of one complete train and three parts of the second split up as the then operation required). The engines would be outside the confines of the passenger area, cutting out smoke nuisance. The approximate estimate of total cost was

Custom Hall, Ocean Terminal, November 1953. Photograph Les Elsey.

given as £471,000, a figure which was to dog the scheme throughout, as is so often the case in matters of this nature. On 30th May 1946 the SR directors approved the scheme at a cost of £475,000.

Within a month 'Suggested Amendments to Architectural Treatment' had surfaced and included a clock tower, enclosed promenade for the sightseeing public, an observation room above the clocks in the tower, lifts to the tower, a decorative coloured glass dome and means of segregating passengers and sightseers all of which, it was claimed, would add 'interest' to the scheme as a whole. It also added to the estimated cost which shot up to £546,000! Three days after these amendments were suggested the Docks and Marine Committee decided that the tower should be

dispensed with, that a suitable similar structure be erected on another site within the docks and that the design of the terminal building (without its tower) be placed before the Royal Fine Art Commission for its observations and suggestions. This body suggested the short end elevations should have the main elevation window treatment carried round and also that there should be - surprise, surprise, a tower at the south end! *Please resubmit on these lines* was the result. On 18th November 1946 the Royal Fine Art Commission gave its blessing to the amended plans but meanwhile the tentacles of bureaucracy were extending to enmesh the scheme.

Times were difficult, and although the war had ended a year before, rationing not only of food but of

building materials was as strict, if not more so, than during hostilities. All manner of bodies had to be consulted for approval to proceed and it was at this point that the whole project got bogged down between the Ministry of Works and the Ministry of Transport. The government had given first priority to John Brown's shipyard and Cunard White Star to renovate the two liners to luxury standards and completely ignored the terminal, being content to let the American tourists wait about in a dingy decaying shed at Southampton.

Between 1st July and 30th September 1946 the project had not advanced at all. When Sir Reginald Hill (Ministry of Transport) telephoned Sir Eustace Missenden on 3rd October to say that the Ministry of Works would oppose the new terminal and that a

That wonderful 'Liner Effect', the Ocean Terminal laying in the water, 1952. Photograph Les Elsey.

30860 LORD HAWKE on a boat train to Waterloo, at the outer platform of the Ocean Terminal, 1 June 1953. Photograph Les Elsey.

repair job on the old sheds should be undertaken, Sir Eustace expressed himself forcefully on the subject to such a degree that Sir Reginald was clearly shaken. Within 24 hours the Ministry of Transport had given their authorisation to the project although it was not subject to a labour priority. With so much damage to housing in Southampton the government did not wish to be accused of diverting labour to luxury building. Additionally, in mid-October, Cunard had resumed sailing to and from the United States.

Instead of one overall contract for the whole building, a series of contracts was thought desirable (possibly to get the work started quickly); the first of these, for piled foundations, was placed early in 1947 and work commenced on site. This procedure, however, did highlight each element of the building, none less so than the fitting out contract which was negotiated with Messrs Maples. This name probably conveyed to the Ministry of Transport visions of grandeur and extravagance. Although the aim was to show the best in British craftsmanship it was at odds with the utility feeling of the time and consequently the MoT demanded great reductions in this part of the building, declaring that buffets and restaurants would not be countenanced. Furthermore, there were other problems on the horizon, such as nationalisation of the railways which would bring with it personnel changes and doubtless an early consideration - or reconsideration - of the

scheme under the new Railway Executive. Fortunately, Sir Eustace Missenden was elevated to the chair of that body so there was in effect a friend at court which ensured that at least there would not be hostility towards the project from that quarter, even if the chairman could not be seen to be leaning too much in favour of one of his own former pet schemes. John Elliot moved up a step at Waterloo, succeeding Sir Eustace, and Biddle remained at Southampton, so there was continuity on the railway side. 1947, however, saw no progress, apart from work on the foundations, for although tenders were received for the various elements of the construction, no approvals for contracts were forthcoming.

Nationalisation of the railways duly came on New Year's day 1948 and shortly afterwards the Ministry of Transport's harbour engineer came up with the absurd proposals to eliminate the heating, flooring, plastering and general finishings to the terminal, leaving just a shell with temporary lighting festooned as a greeting for overseas visitors. On 1st March 1948, the Investments Programmes Committee (how the bureaucrats love these names!) of the MoT conceded such proposals were not feasible and agreed to the work proceeding to the original design, albeit with some modification. In June 1948 the Railway Executive received from Elliot a revised estimate of £775,000 for the building and this meant that the scheme had

to be submitted in its entirety for reauthorisation by the RE and the British Transport Commission.

The escalation of costs was due to various factors, including the sightseers' gallery and tower feature and a new design of gangway - a light alloy telescopic arrangement and probably the first of its type ever to be commissioned. These involved additional research costs and further problems came from low original estimates and increases in labour and material costs, owing to delays in placing contracts. It was not until the end of 1948 that sanction was given to proceed with the completion of the works and even then there were minor setbacks, such as the non-availability of bricks due to housing requirements. Progress was slow but steady during 1949 and it is interesting to read a letter from Elliot to Sir Eustace in July wherein he wrote:

'As you know, the BOAC have provided a new terminal for their flying boats at Southampton Docks and the building has been equipped and furnished in such a manner as to create an excellent impression of the amenities it affords. Although services from and to the United States are not dealt with at this terminal, it would, in my opinion, be invidious to have these two terminal buildings in close proximity to each other, both operated by Nationalised undertakings - one finished off to the last detail and the other spoilt "for a ha'porth of tar"'.

Elliot continued to press this point with his superiors and circum-

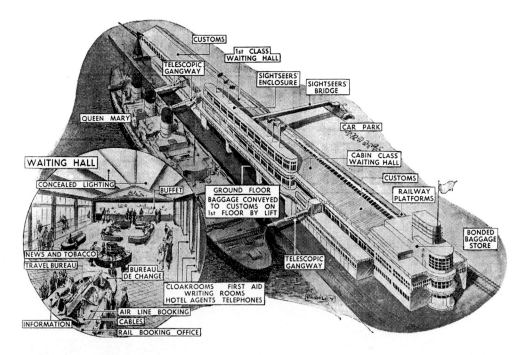

CUSTOMS
1st CLASS WAITING HALL
TELESCOPIC GANGWAY
SIGHTSEERS' ENCLOSURE
SIGHTSEERS' BRIDGE
QUEEN MARY
CAR PARK
CABIN CLASS WAITING HALL
CUSTOMS
RAILWAY PLATFORMS
WAITING HALL
CONCEALED LIGHTING
BUFFET
GROUND FLOOR BAGGAGE CONVEYED TO CUSTOMS ON 1st FLOOR BY LIFT
BONDED BAGGAGE STORE
NEWS AND TOBACCO
TRAVEL BUREAU
BUREAU DE CHANGE
TELESCOPIC GANGWAY
CLOAKROOMS FIRST AID
WRITING ROOMS
HOTEL AGENTS TELEPHONES
AIR LINE BOOKING
CABLES
INFORMATION
RAIL BOOKING OFFICE

vented some restrictions by getting W.H. Smith & Son to provide its own bookstall (agreed to be of a surprisingly high standard when executed) and the Hotels Executive of the BTC to be responsible for the buffet construction. Elliot, however, was translated to the London Midland Region's Chief Regional Officer's chair and C.P. Hopkins succeeded him at Waterloo. By the time the new man arrived he had little more to do than to oversee the opening ceremony arrangements planned for 31st July 1950.

On the day a special all-Pullman train hauled by No.35001 CHANNEL PACKET left Waterloo at 10.10am with the Prime Minister, Minister of Transport, Chairman of BTC and RE and others, arriving at the Ocean Ter-

minal at 11.50am. The Prime Minister, (Rt. Hon. C.R. Attlee) declared the terminal open and unveiled a commemorative plaque after which he went aboard the QUEEN ELIZABETH moored alongside to view the terminal from above. This was followed by luncheon on board (by invitation of Cunard), timed to end at 3.05pm. The special train returned to Waterloo at 3.40pm making a stop at Northam at 3.50pm to pick up the Prime Minister, who had carried out a diversionary programme of short duration in the town. Tea was served en route for a 5.20pm arrival in London.

So, after about four years, the Southern Railway's finest post-war project had come to fruition but not without a tremendous battle by its officers. Normally, in the pre-war

sense, they might have expected completion in about eighteen months and would have had the terminal operational by December 1947, under the banner of the SR. Instead, it was presented to the public more as a BTC/RE venture, as a benefit of nationalisation. Ironically, it did not stay with the Railway Executive for long because on 1st September 1950 it passed into the hands of the Docks and Inland Waterways Executive and so the trains were working into a terminal owned by a non-railway organisation.

For several years especially in the 1950s, traffic prospered but by the next decade air rather than sea liners were becoming the accepted way of crossing the North Atlantic and these machines more than decimated the seaborne traffic. With the withdrawal

Southampton Docks Ocean Terminal

A detail plan of the waiting halls on the first floor

The layout of the ground floor which includes an island platform for accommodating two full-length boat trains at once. Sixteen lifts and two escalators connect this platform with the first floor. The two smaller island platforms at the ends of the building are for passengers travelling by road

THE RAILWAY GAZETTE   August 4, 1950

Southampton Docks Ocean Terminal

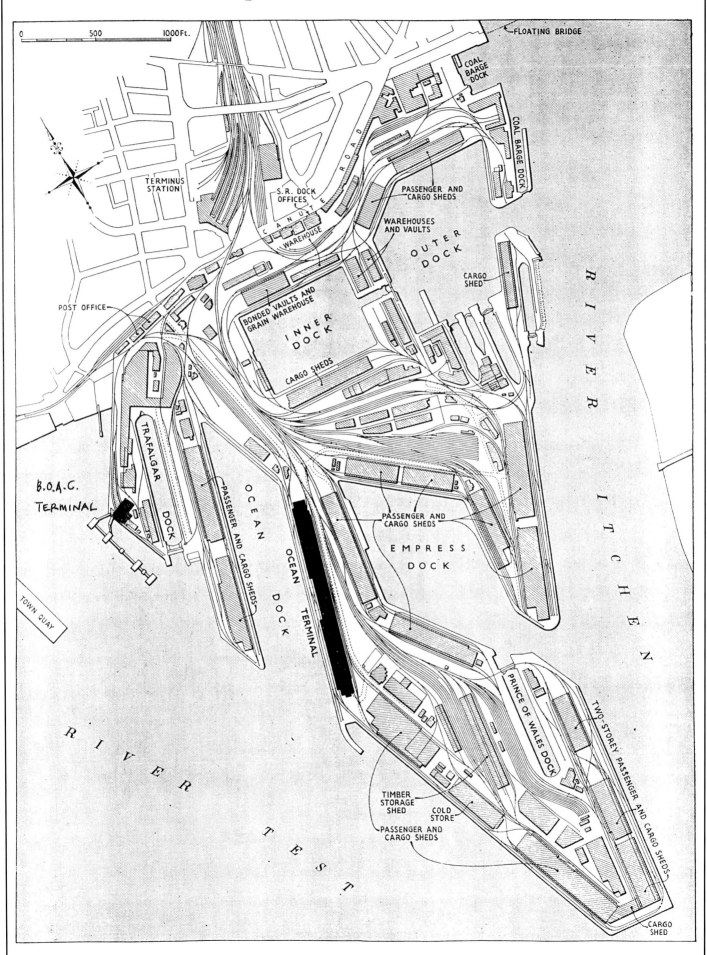

Diagram of Southampton Docks, showing the central position of the new Ocean Terminal

of the Queens and the diversion of the QE2 to cruising, the Ocean Terminal became a white elephant and so was decommissioned at the end of 1980, and demolished in April 1983. In some quarters it was considered to be an engineer-designed rather than architect-designed building but it was none the worse for that and, in retrospect, it was a pity that the one build-

Above. Passenger Lounge, September 1953. Photograph Les Elsey.

ing in the docks which had some character and did not look like a shed had to be destroyed.

BOAC and Berth 50/51

The third station of this review is, as may have been gathered from a foregoing reference, that built for British Overseas Airways Corporation flying boat traffic. Before the war the Empire Air Mail scheme had been inaugurated by Imperial Airways using flying boats based (so far as the United Kingdom was concerned) on Southampton Water. An improvised special train was run for the first, somewhat unexpected, arrival on 15th January 1937; various berths were used at Southampton before war intervened and operations were switched to Poole. With the war over and Imperial Airways long since incorporated into British Overseas Airways Corporation, thoughts turned to having a proper terminal building in Southampton Docks, where passengers would embark on and disembark from the flying boats, with railway connections with London.

Accordingly, agreement was concluded with the Southern Railway for the erection by BOAC of a two-storey passenger handling building at berth 50 and for a railway platform by berth 51, to have a covered way at the southern end of the ramp to connect with the building, thereby affording direct access for passengers off the special airways trains with the terminal. The sole problem at the time was a restriction imposed by the Ministry of Transport that special trains had to have a minimum of 100 passengers. The handling building does not appear to have attracted the same difficulties encountered a few hundred yards away with the Ocean Terminal even though, as Elliot recorded, it was finished to a high standard. Perhaps its lesser size helped. It was brought into use on 31st March 1948.

Official opening junkets took place on 14th April when Lord Nathan, Minister of Civil Aviation, came down from London accompanied by John Elliot in special coaches attached to the 9.30am train from Waterloo. At Southampton Central the two coaches were detached and worked round to arrive at berth 50/51 at 11.45am. Speeches were delivered and allusions made to the building having been provided with its own special platform and siding; hopes were expressed that before long the volume of traffic would justify special trains. At 2.45pm the two coach special train with VIPs on board departed and that, so far as is known, was the sole passenger train ever to grace BOAC's platform at berth 50.

Movement of flying boat passengers on Southampton Water peaked in May 1950 with roughly 60 passengers a day, clearly not enough for one train. The flying boat was in an Indian summer and the last public service at Southampton flew in November 1950. By some peculiar quirk of fate the building and platform survived until recently - though divorced of course, from flying boats.

*****

Such is the tale of one station fulfilling all expectations completion during its one day operational existence, of another fulfilling expectations but for a lesser period than might have reasonably been anticipated and of the third of a trio failing to be of any revenue earning use through no fault of its own.

Bottom left. One-time BOAC building at Southampton Docks, with platform remains at Berth 50/51 on the right.. 14 April 1988. Photograph D.W. Winkworth.

Below. Off 50 Berth, Sunderland G-AKNS CITY OF LIVERPOOL of Aquila Airways. Photograph Les Elsey.

Diesel Dawn

Above. Amongst the most enduring of the BR diesel classes were the rather curious Type 1s from English Electric. They came early on, and were striking indeed, with long sleek 'bonnets' and a thoroughly business-like air. This is D8000, the first of an initial order of twenty, D8000-D8019, which were all intended for BR's 'new' (and first) diesel depot at Devons Road, Bow. See various BRILLs and *Diesel Depots* (Hawkins, Hooper, Reeve, Irwell Press 1989) for details of this depot, a landmark in the modernisation of BR and only demolished in recent years.

Below. D8001 on test at Penrith in 1957. It entered traffic along with D8004 in July - August 1957; *The Railway Magazine* carried a picture of D8007 on a similar test train (at Lancaster) in its November 1957 issue so this may have been the regular 'run-in' for the new 'EE Type 1s', as we learned to call them.

Above. D8001 and attendant staff on the Penrith test. The cab, the makers declared, was 'resiliently mounted on the underframe to reduce noise to a minimum'.

Below. One of the new locos at work, leaving Primrose Hill tunnel on the LNW main line. For many years of course, we were accustomed to seeing the 'Class 20s' in pairs only but in the first years they operated singly, much as the medium size steam locos, 0-6-0s and Moguls, they were intended to replace - on trips and suchlike. They came out only a couple of years on from the 1955 'Pilot Scheme' orders placed late in 1955, and were described at the time as 'Type A'. This early classification (there were 'Type B' and 'Type C' too) soon gave way to the more familiar grading of 1 to 5.

WAR REPORT

ABERDEEN IN THE FRONT LINE

After the Dornier raid of 24th April 1943. The carriage shed, from the damaged roof of the wagon repair shop. Even the granite walls have suffered badly. An adjacent shelter received a direct hit, with loss of life. Photograph J.L. Stevenson Collection.

by J.L. Stevenson

The north-east of Scotland suffered severely from air attack during the Second World War. Yet the experiences of Aberdeen, Peterhead and Fraserburgh have received little publicity and to most people the War experience of Scotland is synonymous with the horrific Clydebank Blitz of April 1941, when after two nights of attacks by massed bombers only a dozen houses in the community were left undamaged. Greenock too suffered badly about the same time and devotees of the Caledonian Railway will recall that Ladyburn engine shed was severely damaged and a Caley Bogie, No.14356, had to be scrapped.

Edinburgh in its key position at the mouth of the Firth of Forth had various scares but was largely unscathed; however, in contrast great havoc was wrought on Aberdeen, Peterhead and Fraserburgh. Enemy aircraft were constantly patrolling the North Sea, carrying bombs, and if shipping did not present suitable targets Aberdeen and the seaside towns to its north and south were the recipients

of these bombs - and not all these locations were heavily defended.

Aberdeen itself suffered some thirty air raids, the first in June 1940 and the last - and much the most serious - in April 1943. The targets hit were largely residential property but the Hall Russell shipyard became an early victim. The first significant damage on railway property occurred on 31st October 1940 when a high explosive bomb fell at the north end of Kittybrewster shed. The raid seems to have been a fairly small affair with other bombs dropped indiscriminately on such scarcely vital targets as a cemetery and a bowling green, while the Beach Dance Hall had a narrow escape.

Kittybrewster shed, being a roundhouse, would naturally appeal to the German crews, familiar with such installations, as a worthwhile target. The main victim of the attack was one of the little Class Z4 0-4-2 tanks, No.6843, the rear end of which happened to be sticking out of the shed. It appeared to have received very nearly a direct hit, for the cab and bunker were largely destroyed and the rear of

the engine thrown into the air. It lived to fight another day, being repaired in due course at Inverurie; it later became BR 68190 and was not withdrawn until April 1960. On the adjacent running line, having apparently been en route to or from the turntable, 4-4-0 No.6854 SOUTHESK was standing left standing minus its tender. The engine seems to have avoided serious damage although the tender may well have been less fortunate. Behind No.6843, and within the shed, was G10 0-4-4T No.6887, while on adjacent shed roads were a B12 4-6-0 and a J72 0-6-0T, No.542. All apparently little the worse. Fortunately, the turntable appears to have been still operational and, despite severe damage to the roof over four roads these could quickly be put back into use.

Many of the raids had been in the tip and run category but by far the most serious and destructive attack took place in the late evening of 21st April 1943, when 25 Dornier 217s flew across the North Sea from Stavanger with Aberdeen as their prime target. Over 50 bombs were dropped on the city, causing immense destruction

The result of the HE bomb on Kittybrewster shed, 31st October 1940. Z4 No.6843 has received most of the blast and lies upended with its bunker and cab crumpled like a toy. On the right is 4-4-0 No.6854 SOUTHESK minus its tender, the engine apparently undamaged. Photograph J.L. Stevenson Collection.

mainly to residential property, some 8,000 houses being damaged. There was heavy loss of life.

Once again Kittybrewster received attention, mainly to the yard on the east side of the station, but the carriage shed and wagon repair shop lying between the station and the engine shed (which seems to have escaped damage) were also largely destroyed.

By all accounts, the Aberdonians were characteristically matter of fact in their response to air raids such as this. The response of one north easter was quoted at the time: *'Aye we can stick it. Fit else is there tae dee?'* History does not relate what

Kitty thought of these catastrophic affairs. That the lady really existed is borne out by a plaque in a nearby hotel which, if memory serves, recalls that *'She was a kindly canty dame and they called her Kitty Brewster.'*

In contrast to Kittybrewster no significant damage seems to have been suffered by the LMS shed,

Kittybrewster roundhouse later on 31st October 1940, with some order restored and the Z4 put back on an even keel. J72 No.542 stands ready for service as if little had happened. The shed roof has been shored up. Photograph J.L. Stevenson Collection.e full cover restored. Photograph J.L. Stevenson Collection.

Ferryhill, at the south end. Situated on the southern outskirts of the city adjoining Duthie Park, it must have appeared a less attractive target. But damage to the adjacent Dee viaduct would have been an effective strike. Further south in August 1941 the South Esk viaduct at Montrose, a single line structure carrying the main line, had its third span at the south end damaged by a bomb which appears to have passed through the lattice work. Mercifully the Forth and Tay bridges survived intact, though sporadic attacks were made on the former.

Right. One would have expected the Z4 tank to be scrapped after its misadventure but these were useful engines, and 6843 awaits attention in Inverurie works yard, bereft of cab, bunker and trailing axle. It had a further twenty years of service before it. Photograph J.L. Stevenson Collection.

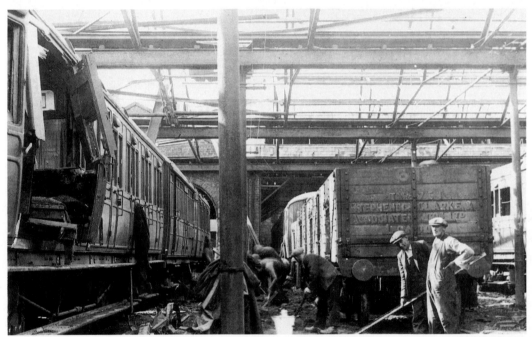

Left. After the major air raid on 24th April 1943 the carriage shed at Kittybrewster lies open to the elements, with considerable damage to rolling stock. Photograph J.L. Stevenson Collection.

Below. Some three years after the damage of October 1940 the end of the shed still bore the scars of battle. The roof coverage has been reduced and conditions overhead appear far from secure. A few years later the structure had been made good and the full cover restored. Photograph J.L. Stevenson Collection.

Rotherham in South Yorkshire long ago merged into Sheffield to form a massive conurbation. The town is associated with the steel industry and to this day rail travellers ride past the two major works at Templeborough and Park Gate, the latter still retaining a small internal fleet of diesel shunters. It is not generally realised that Rotherham was once a railway town, with the legendary Isaac Dodds building about seventy locomotives at his Holmes Engine Works between 1838 and 1866; Owen & Dyson manufactured railway wheels and axles and from 1861 the well known Harrison & Camm built thousands of wagons. Wagon construction and repair was also carried out in the town, by the North Central Wagon Company, the British Wagon Company and the Great Central Railway. Furthermore, the town could once boast three stations. The Westgate terminus lay at the end of a branch which ran down from Holmes Junction, with the former trackbed used to this day as part of the sidings of the well known scrap merchant C.F. Booth Ltd (no relation). Rotherham Central is close to the town centre and has been re-opened as the town's only station. Rotherham Masborough was situated on the Midland line and is seen in this view of 30th June 1966. 'Crosti' 9F No.92029 had arrived with a lengthy train of steel flats and was standing beside the water column awaiting signals. Brush Type 2s Nos.D5848 and D5832 passed through with empty mineral wagons and headed off down the freight-only line towards Canklow and Beighton. Minutes later the signals cleared and the 'Crosti' was given the road to cross over and follow the same route as the Type 2s.

ROTHERHAM - LAST DAYS OF STEAM
Photographs and Captions by Adrian Booth

This view was taken from the footbridge alongside Holmes Junction signal box and, although six years after the end of steam, is included to show the track layout in the area. The track behind the photographer runs to Sheffield Midland whilst the main tracks curve left into Masborough station. Holmes sidings are on the left, where a 350hp shunter was always employed. The tracks at right curve off to Masborough South Junction whilst the bridge at extreme right takes the C.F. Booth Ltd. siding (formerly Westgate station branch) under the freight only line. The date is 30th May 1974 with Type 2 diesel 25043 heading a Leeds to Birmingham train.

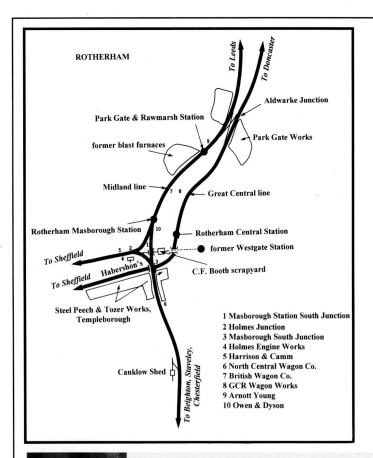

ROTHERHAM

To Leeds
To Doncaster

Aldwarke Junction

Park Gate & Rawmarsh Station

former blast furnaces

Park Gate Works

Midland line

Great Central line

Rotherham Masborough Station

Rotherham Central Station

former Westgate Station

To Sheffield

C.F. Booth scrapyard

Habershon's

To Sheffield

Steel Peech & Tozer Works,
Templeborough

1 Masborough Station South Junction
2 Holmes Junction
3 Masborough South Junction
4 Holmes Engine Works
5 Harrison & Camm
6 North Central Wagon Co.
7 British Wagon Co.
8 GCR Wagon Works
9 Arnott Young
10 Owen & Dyson

Canklow Shed

To Beighton, Staveley,
Chesterfield

Above. These days Rotherham is associated with the well known scrapyard of C.F. Booth Ltd where large numbers of BR diesel locomotives have been cut up. In steam days a small scrapyard was located on the west side of the Midland line, just to the north of Parkgate & Rawmarsh station. A small number of engines were cut there, in Arnott Young's yard, including 4F No.44339 and an ex-Southern trio of 2-6-2Ts Nos.84013, 84019 and 84026. On 25th July 1967 two 9Fs, 92030 and 92065 were photographed against the backdrop of Park Gate blast furnaces.

Top left. Towards the very end of steam the Eastern Region allocated Departmental numbers 17 - 32 to a fleet of B1s used for carriage heating duties. Two examples were quite regularly seen at Holmes Yard, Nos.30 (61050) and 32 (61315), both transferred to Departmental stock in February 1966. No.30 was in action on 21st October 1967 steaming past Masborough Station South Junction box. When not in use it was often to be seen stabled at Canklow or Barrow Hill sheds.

Left. The town's engine shed was at Canklow, latterly coded 41D, on the west side of the Beighton to Rotherham freight-only line, about two miles south of Masborough station. In the 1960s it played host to a mixture of LMS/LNER/BR types, accommodated in five sidings and a brick built roundhouse. Diesels only infiltrated to any extent in the mid-1960s.

Above. Departmental 32 (61315) seen on 14th November 1967 having steamed up from Canklow and then reversing back past Holmes crossing on its way into Holmes Yard. The building on the left is part of the Habershon's works, a well known local company, who had their own siding up to 1965 upon which they operated a Barclay saddle tank for over thirty years.

Below. The tanks were later moved from Canklow to stand in the sidings at Holmes. 41708 (Derby 1880) was positioned separately from the others and in this 11th February 1967 view, has a bag over its chimney. It must surely be a great source of regret to preservationists that one of the Deeley dock tanks and both the 47000 locos (both long and short saddle tank designs) were not saved. Sadly, all went for scrap and these designs passed into history.

Above. It is well documented that Staveley steel works near Chesterfield had a 99 year lease whereby the main line company supplied steam engines to undertake the works shunting. It is perhaps less well known that when the lease expired the loco fleet was sent for storage to Canklow shed. I first saw them on 7th December 1965 when 41528, 41533, 41708, 41734, 41763, 41804, 41835, 47001 and 47005 were lined up on the two sidings on the road side of the coaling stage. They caused quite a stir amongst local spotters at the time, being considerable rarities, and quite a change from the usual diet of B1s, 8Fs, K1s, 9Fs, WDs and so on. 41533 stands in front of the Canklow coal stage on 7th December 1965.

The Sheer Wonder of it All...

There are many classic views associated with particular spots on the steam railway, particularly sheds. The 'aerial' views of Brighton, Worcester snd Aberbeeg spring to mind, for such shots were often too obvious to miss for many visiting photographers. All sheds had their vantage points, familiar to the *cognoscenti* but unknown to the rest of us. Willesden from the canal was one and so was Old Oak, from the same canal, but they do not appear in the photographic record - unless someone out there has the prints to prove otherwise? Sheds were strange entities, and whether surrounded by open fields or close-packed terrace hoses, the view 'from the outside in' is very rare indeed. By this I don't mean the overall view such as the Brighton ones mentioned above, but the 'as you walked in' sort of insight - that elusive effect of peering over the fence or through the gate, to capture that magic urchin's moment of 'casing the joint'. *British Railways Illustrated* would be very

pleased indeed to hear from anyone who has such photos incidentally.... This is a classic, taken by Peter Gray at 7am on a Sunday morning, 6 May 1956, peering over at the engine lines at Bristol Barrow Road shed. The old Midland roundhouse looms on the left and the King, 6024 KING EDWARD I stands amongst various LM and Standard types. All of them are robustly in steam but the King is dead and bereft of its front driving wheels. It had been a bad year for the King - the 'Bogie Crisis' earlier that year had seen it laid up at its home shed, Old Oak and now here it was again, similarly incarcerated. For some reason it was not dealt with at the Western's Bath Road shed, though it was officially booked in there for this period, according to the Swindon records - see *Peto's Register Volume 1*. Photograph Peter Gray.

Gidea Park, launch pad (well almost) for the widening on to Shenfield. This is looking east towards Shenfield, through Bridge 106. This was one of the bridges 'cut in two' and the work can be readily made out, from the differences in the brickwork. The original two track main line ran through the right hand arch (carrying Brentwood Road) whilst the left hand was a single arch spanning only a single track line, giving access to one or two sidings opposite Romford Wagon Sheet Factory. A 'twinning' of the bridge gave two similar arches, one for each set of two tracks. The original arch dated from the 1840s and great care was necessary to ensure against settlement. The angle of skew was 51° and heavy timbering was used and maintained until the new arch was turned and backed up for one third of its height in concrete. The Goods Shed (the Romford Factory lies behind it) stands high on the right; the new sidings (see plan) run off under the new arch, to the left. 3 February 1932.

The Gidea Park - Shenfield Widening
'Half a Million Cubic Yards of Essex Have Been Removed'

Notes *by M Fry*

'An Important Railway Widening' was in the offing, the railway press announced in the early days of 1931. The Nation was deeply mired in economic slump, and one response had been the Government funding of big railway capital projects. The idea, in part, was to finance works that had long been desirable but for which the railway companies had not had sufficient wherewithal. By this means, it was hoped, would unemployment figures be dented, or at least their inexorable rise be slowed. The long overdue upgrading and enlarging of the old Great Eastern main line out into Essex was deemed a suitable case for treatment. In the previous year good progress had been made on widening between Romford and Gidea Park (actually as far as Romford Factory, a little to the east of Gidea Park station - see photographs), with two miles of double track being enlarged to four. Just these two miles involved 4$\frac{1}{2}$ million bricks, 31,500 cubic yards of concrete, 10$\frac{1}{4}$ miles of single track, two overbridges and five underbridges, 1,400 tons of rails, and 22,000 sleepers. The project, if it was to continue to its logical con-

clusion, was going to consume a fair portion of whatever Government money was available.

These widening works, from Romford to Gidea Park/Romford Factory, set the scene for the widening on to Shenfield. A contract had been let in January 1930, commencing about 30 chains west of Romford station (where the then existing four lines from London converged into two) and terminating about 54 chains east of Gidea Park station - effectively Romford Factory. Thus would the four tracks extend to a point east of Gidea Park. The works had been completed by September 1931 and were made up of the following:

Laying down two additional tracks on the down side.
Provision of extra sidings east of Gidea Park station.
Enlargement of the goods yards on the south side of Romford station.
Rebuilding Romford station.
Improvements at Gidea Park station.
Widening of the existing bridges under and over the railway.
The whole of the project amounted to 2 miles 22 chains, and extended from the London end of Romford station to Gidea Park/Romford Factory, which

point then formed the boundary with the widening we are concerned with here, Gidea Park to Shenfield.

Firm news of the 'Important Railway Widening', first noted earlier in the year (above) was unveiled in the July 31 1931 issue of *The Railway Gazette*: *'The LNER announce that work is shortly to be commenced on widening the main line between Gidea Park and Shenfield. The work of reconstructing Romford station and laying additional tracks for two miles in the vicinity of Romford is now nearly complete; the new scheme provides for the construction of two additional lines from Gidea Park/Romford Factory to Shenfield, a distance of six miles , and will give the LNER main Ipswich line four tracks continuously for the first 20 miles out of Liverpool Street to Shenfield. The existing stations at Harold Wood, Brentwood, and Shenfield will be altered and improved, and a burrowing junction from the down main line to the Southend line is to be made at Shenfield. The LNER has obtained a Government grant under the Development (Loan Guarantees and Grants) Act for the relief of unemployment for these works.'*

This final stage of the GE main line widening, what we call the Gidea Park

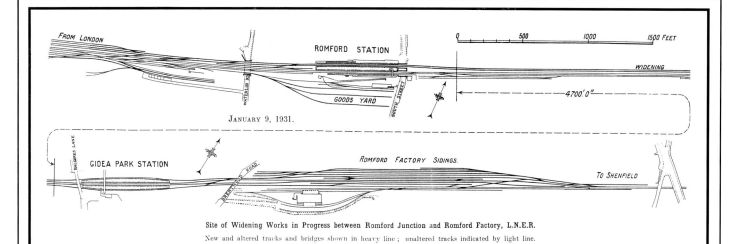

Site of Widening Works in Progress between Romford Junction and Romford Factory, L.N.E.R.

New and altered tracks and bridges shown in heavy line; unaltered tracks indicated by light line.

PRECURSOR. Extract with kind permission, *The Railway Gazette*. The plan represents the GE main line widening, Romford to Gidea Park (actually Romford Junction - Romford Factory), which was the predecessor of the Gidea Park - Shenfield work. The date is 9 January 1931 and the work saw completion by November that year. It enabled the LNER to run local services to and from Gidea Park almost independently of the main line traffic. It was only the penultimate stage of the Grand Design, and but the springboard for the subject of this article, the widening onwards to the junction of the Southend line, beyond Shenfield.

- Shenfield Widening, was soon under way. Work began in February 1932; 'Half a million cubic yards of Essex will have been removed', the LNER anticipated, when work over the $6^1/_2$ mile main between Gidea Park and Shenfield was completed. Carrying forward the widening of the tracks in the neighbourhood of Romford, the Gidea Park - Shenfield project would make four lines of metals available all the way from Liverpool Street to the junction with the Southend line at Shenfield, enabling local service trains to travel on separate lines without interference to express services between Colchester, Southend and London. Part of the scheme was the construction of a new single line of railway one mile long on the down side at Shenfield, passing *under* the Colchester main lines and forming a 'burrowing' junction with the down Southend line three-quarters of a mile beyond Shenfield Junction. Three LNER stations, Harold Wood, Brentwood and Shenfield were to be rebuilt. Altogether twenty two new and altered bridges were involved, and to avoid excessive excavation through the Brentwood cutting it was necessary to construct retaining walls, which rose to twenty feet in some parts, for a total length of nearly two miles. These great walls formed a distinctive feature of the Widening, and were made in what was then termed 'mass concrete'. New embankments, *The Railway Gazette* recorded, would 'absorb 284,500 cubic yards and the new railway will absorb 110,000 cubic yards of material.'

The engineering features of the Gidea Park - Shenfield Widening were not spectacular but they were formi-

Gidea Park, looking east through the station, under Bridge 104, towards Shenfield, 3 February 1932. The work here of course was part of the Romford - Gidea Park widening, the one previous to 'our' one - Gidea Park - Shenfield. The principles involved, of course, were the same. Bridge 104 looks unchanged (unlike Bridge 106); the station had lines running round the island platforms and these arches were pre-existing, for the tracks to regain the two track main line. So here it was a question of easing back the cutting sides. There were already high retaining walls underneath each of the 'outside' arches. As the two island platforms already existed little work was necessary for them to take the new alignment. The change wrought is summarised thus: Down Loop - Down Main - Up Main - Up Loop became Down Local - Up Local - Down Through - Up Through - that is, the two middle ones 'reversed direction'. The station's opening, as 'Squirrels Heath (for Gidea Park)' was reported in a 1911 issue of the *Great Eastern Magazine*..

This view is east of the previous one, looking towards London and Gidea Park station; the Goods Shed rises up in a mist of smoke, with the Romford Factory on the left. The paucity of sidings before the Widening is noticeable (view is before the work - on 29 March 1930) and the inscription *BRIDGE No107* reveals the presence of a brook - it ran north to south (right to left) under the main line (only two tracks still, of course) and round the back of the Romford Factory.

dable - if workmanlike. It was a question of 'adjusting' the bridges and earthworks to take two extra sets of tracks. Embankments had to be broadened, cuttings opened out, and bridges altered to suit. Termed the 'Second Stage of Main Line Widening between Romford and Shenfield' it was described in the *LNER Magazine* in 1933. The point was made that the stretch

from Gidea Park to Shenfield included the long heavy gradient from Harold Wood past Brentwood up to Ingrave, well known (not least as a favourite of the Great Eastern for its 'official views') as Brentwood Bank. For the eastern half of its length it ran in the long, deep cutting referred to above.

A good part of the heaviest work in connection with the Gidea Park -

Shenfield Widening was concentrated on this Brentwood Bank cutting, for it involved the building of retaining walls on each side, avoiding the removal, thereby, of hundreds of thousand of cubic yards of excavation.

The most complex 'adjustment' work to a single structure in the Gidea Park - Shenfield Widening probably concerned 'Seven Arch Bridge', a grace-

The new layout at Romford Factory, viewed from Bridge 106 and looking east, towards the site of the photograph above. New four track layout shown to good effect. New carriage sidings lay beyond the signal box and the newish ballast, clean brickwork of the retaining wall and bright concrete of the engine pits reveal the extent of the new work. The original lines remain as before on the right - the new local lines were added on the left. The N7 0-6-2T is No.2625 and carries a FENCHURCH ST destination board for its return to London. Construction of these engine pits 'stole' twenty or more yards from the houses backing onto the line, visible on the left. They fronted Brentwood Road, shown crossing the road on Bridge 106 in the top photograph, page 72. February 1932.

The point, more or less, at which the Gidea Park - Shenfield Widening began lay a few yards west of Bridge 109. It was replaced by the Southend Arterial Road in 1925 - this is it, eerily empty. It was denoted Bridge 108A, because its predecessor 109 (just visible on the left - that is, towards London) was due for removal. It was stripped back to the arch crown and blown up one Sunday during 1933, with the rubble simply cleared off the (then) two track main line. 28 February 1925.

ful structure fifty foot high above Brentwood Bank. It had tall slim piers, originally constructed with a void or gap through the centre of each pier. The two new tracks were placed one each side of the existing tracks through the cutting - the existing two tracks passed through the main central span. The cutting had to be widened out and the new tracks were taken each side of the central span - the piers alongside needed substantial underpinning, and the contractors accomplished this by bricking in the voids and adding 45° struts.

The foundations of other bridges also had to be strengthened by underpinning. Much of the rest of the work, apart from all the spoil removal,

was mainly the extending and widening of existing bridges or putting new ones 'in place of old'. Each of the twenty two bridges was a problem in its own right, according to whether it passed over or under the railway, and had to be dealt with in its own way. A number were demolished by explosives. 'Some have been blown to pieces' the LNER Magazine revealed - such as 109, blown up after a new bridge, 108A, was constructed to take the new Southend Arterial. Others were cut in two, one half continuing to function, while part of the new structure was built on the site of the half which had gone, being subsequently removed when no longer required. In one case the bridge which

was to carry the Widening was built first, and the existing tracks temporarily slewed over on to it, to give a clear field for the contractors to rebuild the old structure. 'In yet another instance', The LNER Magazine (and The Railway Gazette) recorded '...as the lines cannot be moved, a temporary bridge was constructed formed of the permanent girders of another bridge not yet built, to carry for the time being the new lines over the existing brick arch with which it is not sage to take liberties, and while the trains continue to pass over the temporary structure, the old arch underneath it will be stripped and dropped into the roadway below to allow the new permanent steel superstructure - which meanwhile will be constructed alongside - to be drawn into its final resting place.'

The new Avoiding Line to the Southend Branch passed under the main line east of Shenfield, and temporary decking was put up, to carry the main lines while the new abutments

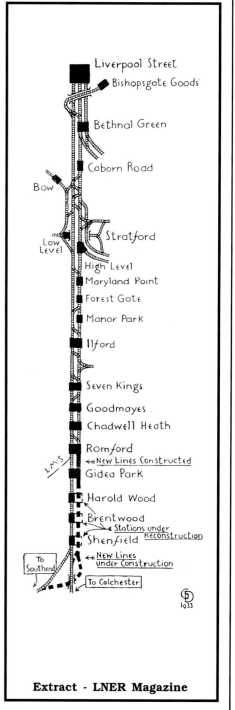

Extract - LNER Magazine

The Gidea Park - Shenfield Widening transformed three stations, Harold Wood, Brentwood and Shenfield. Each, until then, was very much a Great Eastern product - rather rambling affairs often with the slightly embarrassed air of a sleepy country backwater thrust into the creeping metropolitan orbit of London. This is the 'forecourt' at Harold Wood, 9 September 1931. The GE could sometimes carry dull probity to extremes.... TO LONDON inscribed on the print places the view. This is the south (up) side of the line, viewed from the conjunction of three roads - Oak Road and Fitzilian Avenue running parallel to the line and Athelstan Road at right angles to the GE main line.

The country station feel of Harold Wood disappeared on the widening. This is the down side in September 1922, before some long overdue platform renewal work was carried out. The two tracks *are* the Great Eastern main line.

were constructed in trenches below. In any widening or railway work of this nature, there were places where land proved difficult to get, and/or the compensation which had to be paid for disturbance was unduly high. In such instances the LNER Land Department took care that only the very minimum area that would serve was acquired. On the Gidea Park - Shenfield Widening the material excavated was mainly a mixture of silty clay and sand, a de-

posit which proved particularly treacherous in the presence of water. The slopes of the cuttings and embankments had therefore to be made relatively flat, usually not less than one in three - every three feet measured horizontally meant a drop or rise of one foot in the slope. Such proportions demand a lot of land and in this 'up and coming' district, where land prices were high, such profligacy was out of the question. On these stretches it

was necessary to make up the embankments with ashes and dry filling specially brought for the purpose. The slopes in these parts could then be made much steeper, reducing in great part the area of land which would otherwise have had to be purchased. In this way, heavy claims for compensation were avoided.

For much of the Gidea Park - Shenfield Widening the old GE slopes had been badly affected by slips, and at one time or another costly measures to stop the earth movements, by providing drains and retaining walls, had been carried out. Where such action had been taken the ground had stabilised, and could carry the weight of the material in the widened embankments. Only in one or two places did trouble arise, with fresh movement in the old slips, set off by the added weight. This necessitated special remedial work. In the case of the new surfaces of the cuttings many drains were necessary - wherever it seemed that trouble might arise through the presence of water in the subsoil.

There were three stations on the Gidea Park - Shenfield Widening, Harold Wood, Brentwood and Shenfield - which were extensively remodelled and provided with new buildings as necessary. Some parts of the old stations remained, and the new structures were 'designed to be in conformity with the old buildings.' (They certainly weren't to my eye.)

The principal structural alterations at the stations were radical; provision was made, for instance, for the up platform at Harold Wood to be lengthened and new island and down line platforms of the same length provided. At Brentwood the down line platform was to be extended to 600 feet

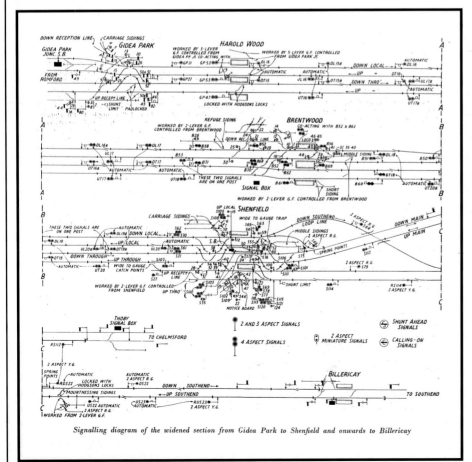

Signalling diagram of the widened section from Gidea Park to Shenfield and onwards to Billericay

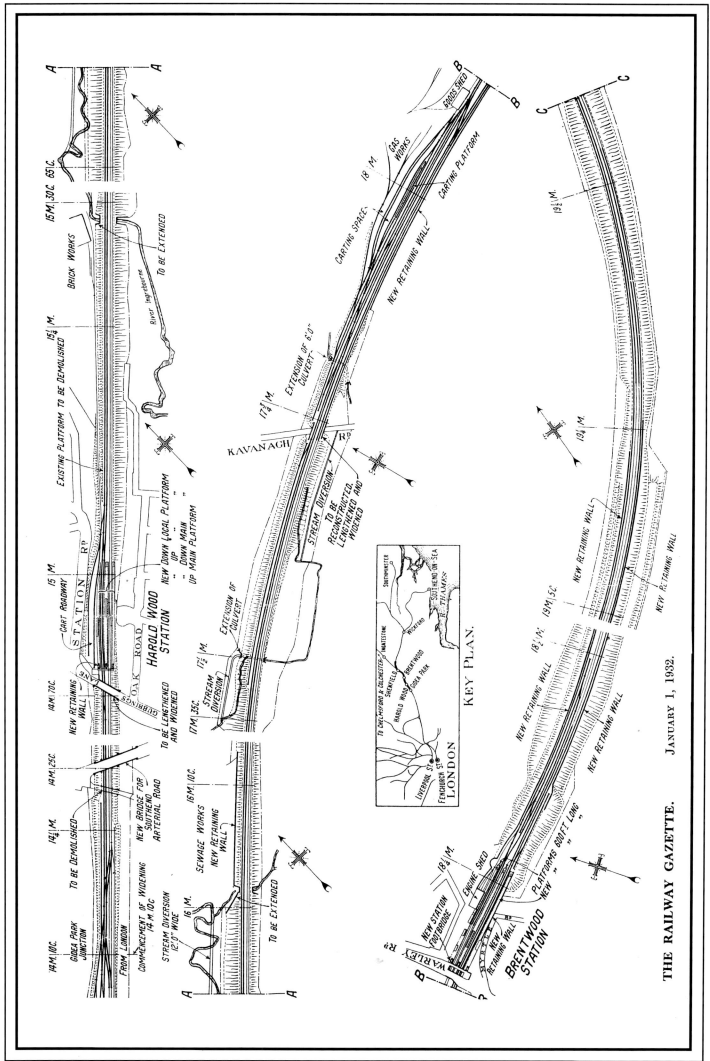

THE RAILWAY GAZETTE.   JANUARY 1, 1932.

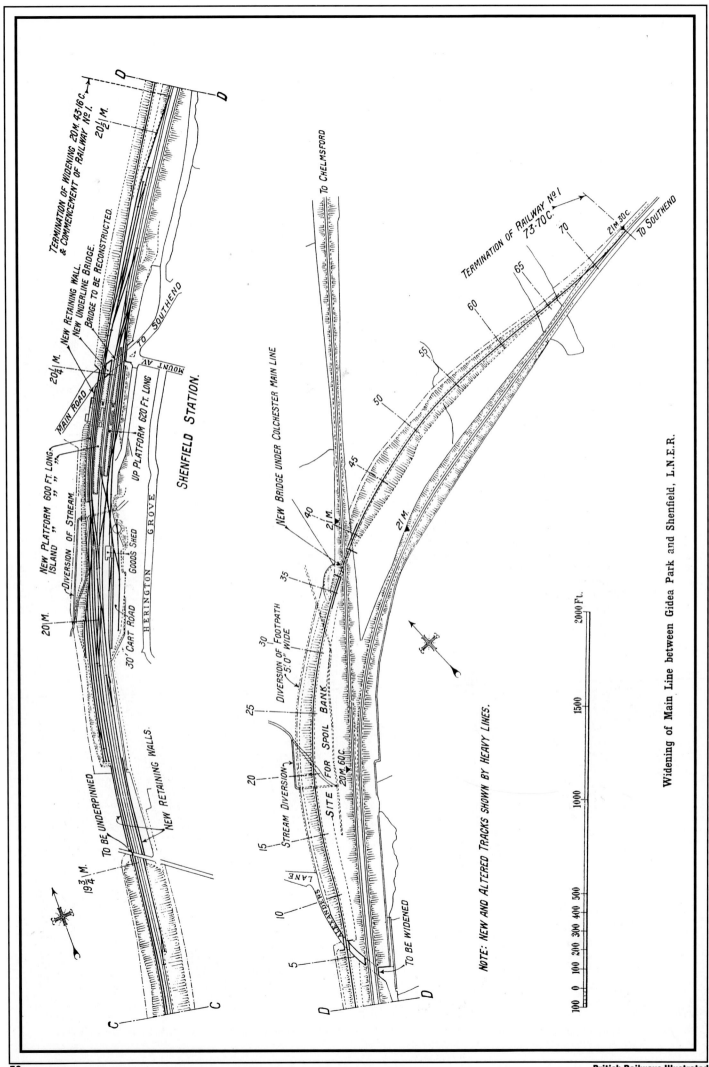

Widening of Main Line between Gidea Park and Shenfield, L.N.E.R.

NOTE: NEW AND ALTERED TRACKS SHOWN BY HEAVY LINES.

The down side at Harold Wood hid a most peculiar feature - this long siding which dropped down and ran for some distance to a brickworks, some distance off in the then more or less empty 'urban district of Hornchurch'. The little bridge is the passenger access to the down side building shown in the photograph page 76. View is looking east.

and the existing up platform became an island of 600 feet, the same length as the additional platform for the up side. At Shenfield the up platform was extended to 620 feet, the existing down platform transformed into an island and a new platform provided on the down side. The subway at Shenfield was also lengthened.

The *LNER Magazine* looked forward to finishing the project 'by the end of 1933'. Completion of the work, the magazine felt, *'should give opportunities for many experiments in train running on the old Great Eastern main line between Liverpool Street and Colchester, which already carries a very heavy traffic, particularly in the summer months.'*

****

The Gidea Park Widening opened to traffic on January 1 1934. Its two ad-

ditional tracks totalled 6 miles 30 chains and took in the three stations noted above - Harold Wood, Brentwood and Shenfield. All three, more or less, were new stations.

There was a complete colour light resignalling, from Gidea Park to beyond Shenfield both on the main line and the Southend branch. Two new boxes were built, Brentwood and Shenfield, and this enabled five older

The Harold Wood staggered platforms and the footbridge before widening, on 9 September 1931. View is towards Shenfield, from the up side. The down side and its buildings lie beyond.

boxes, Harold Wood, Brentwood Station, Brentwood Yard, Ingrave and Shenfield, to be dispensed with. There had also been two new boxes in 1931, Romford and Gidea Park. The signalling between the interlockings at Gidea Park, Brentwood and Shenfield was automatic. (In 1928 two automatic sections on the down line and one on the up line had been introduced, thereby enabling a signalbox to be closed between Harold Wood and Brentwood, and this working was covered in the new scheme.)

The signalling provided for a traffic headway of three minutes, laid out to suit a future (d.c.) electrification. The 'searchlight' signals had a high 'candlepower' and an intense beam was derived from low wattage lamps, the colour being produced by moving a small spectacle (carrying red, yellow and green glass roundels) in the line of the beam between the reflector and the lens system. The movement of the coloured spectacle was governed by an electromagnetic system controlled from the relevant signal lever. To provide sufficient warning of approach to a stop signal for high speed trains a fourth aspect was necessary, and to obtain this a separate lamp unit giving a yellow aspect was fixed above the searchlight unit. This separate unit projected the same beam candle power as the searchlight unit, and was lit when the signal ahead showed a single yellow aspect. The sequence of aspects behind a train was red, yellow, double yellow, green.

'Widening' doesn't really do justice to the extent of the work. Add in all the other widening on the old Great Eastern main line and it made for a monumental undertaking, unequalled until the great electrifications began decades later.

Thanks to Peter Kay for advice in the preparation of this article - a photographic record of the work follows in the next sixteen pages.

Top. A lovely panorama of the classic GE station - offset platforms, signal box and a truly local goods yard concerned with coal for domestic hearths. Delivered round about by horse and cart, of course. 9 September 1931.

Below. Complete transformation. The modern Harold Wood station, a few weeks after completion of the widening - widening done on the down side, old lines relatively untouched at the right. View is from the new replacement footbridge, east towards Shenfield, on 19 January 1934.

Middle above. Gubbins Lane was carried on Bridge 110 across the main line at the London end of Harold Wood station. It had not previously provided any access to the station, which had been independently arrived at for up and down sides, as shown in the previous photographs. The new 'village school' architecture adopted for the new stations of the Widening was, ideally, placed at the 'head' of a site such as Harold Wood, passengers passing through one set of offices to the platforms, whether by footbridge or subway. The new brickwork reveals how Gubbins Lane had been rebuilt for four tracks rather than two. October 1933.

Above. View from platform level, up at the new station building, late 1933. Only a few signs and the lamps need to go in. Beyond the new footbridge (hardly an aesthetic improvement over the previous bridge - *see photograph bottom page 79* - but more practicable for the working of the new station) is the rebuilt Gubbins Lane bridge. The high retaining walls are a notable feature, made necessary by the cutting at this point.

Below. Harold Wood platform buildings, looking east, 19 January 1934.

Above. 'Village School' architecture - Harold Wood booking Office, 19 April 1934. The sign says, below a loose interpretation of a K3 Mogul, *THE LNER CAN SOLVE YOUR FREIGHT TRANSPORT AS EFFECTIVELY AS THE MAGIC CARPET SOLVED THOSE OF PRINCE HUSSEIN.*

Below. Another semi-rural idyll, Brentwood station (up side - London to left, Shenfield to right) on 10 September 1931. Like Harold Wood, there were separate buildings on both up and down side.

Above. Down side and cab rank at Brentwood, 10 September 1931.

Below. View from the footbridge at Brentwood, looking east into the great Brentwood Bank, 10 September 1931. Down side is to the left, with the cab rank shown in the photograph above. Tucked in the corner at the station's country end is the engine shed, its rear wall just visible. The signal box is a GE Type 2 (for this very useful classification system, see *The Signal Box*, the Signalling Study Group, OPC 1986), dating back to the original interlocking of the station.

Above. Brentwood station from the east end. The lines were pretty cramped here and the difficult brief was to provide four lines *and* retain the engine shed (the three road building close by the down platform). The widening at Brentwood was done wholly on the up side, with the old Down Main and Up Main left as before. The down platform was lengthened by a hundred feet, bringing it way past the engine shed - the turntable in front of it had been removed some time before. While the shed itself is long gone, the curious semi-circle of brickwork which accommodated the turntable can be seen there still. The up platform, central in this view, was converted to an island and also lengthened, and a new platform built on the up side - that is, on the left of this view.

Below. An illustration of just how very awkwardly constrained the GE main line was. This is Bridge 121 carrying Warley Road at the west (London) end of Brentwood station. The new station buildings were put up here, and the entrance was to be from Warley Road. This ancient bridge was clearly unsuitable and, standing in the way of progress as few others did in the Widening, it was replaced by a longer and altogether wider structure, for vehicles to pick up and set down. 14 September 1931.

Above. The old goods yard at Brentwood, from the northern approach to the Warley Road bridge, looking towards London, 14 September 1931. The goods shed, a wonderful GE amalgam which had grown up over generations, survived the Widening, for the new tracks were placed on the south side of the main line over to the left in this view. For that purpose, it was necessary to buy up the entire Victoria Road terrace (the washing is highly visible in the back gardens) from the Ecclesiastical Commissioners.

Below. Brentwood goods yard, from the steps of the Yard Box, a print suitably labelled in contemporary GE/LNER fashion. The buildings of the Brentwood Gas Co. rear up on the left; much of the layout on that side remained unaltered but the gardens of Cromwell Road (right) lost ten yards or so.

Above. Finishing touches to the new station building at Brentwood, 19 January 1934 - some days after official inauguration of the Widening. The sign at a drunken angle in the corner of the building, above the car, announces the contractor to be Longden & Son Ltd, 'Builders & Public Work Contractors Sheffield'.

Below. Brentwood - the finished station, 27 February 1934. The complete transformation effected can be appreciated from a comparison with the photograph on page 84 *(top)*. Note old buildings (still there today) on Down Local platform.

Above. Down on the platforms at 'Brentwood and Warley', 27 February 1934. View is from the up side, looking towards Shenfield.

Below. The completed station building. 'Chapelesque' is one summation of the style employed. The design is still attractive today, though the building has suffered indifference and unsympathetic signing and painting.

The 'new style' edifice, brand new, at Brentwood,
February 1934. The new footbridge is alongside;
the steps lead up to Warley Road.

Above. The attractiveness of the styling was enhanced by placing complementary structures either side of the bridge. Inevitably, there was a W.H. Smith & Son's bookstall. 19 April 1934.

Below. Brentwood signal box, 26 June 1934. Considerations of site and space made for tall and narrow boxes - at Brentwood there were three floors and a store below. On the first floor was the relay room and on the second floor the electric circuit breakers. On the top was the mechanical frame, illuminated track diagram and the usual signal box equipment.

The prospect eastwards, 19 April 1934. The heavy concrete retaining walls were made necessary through the treacherous nature of the soil - otherwise a far greater area of land would have to have been acquired. The 'Great Wall of Brentwood' had a total length of 2½ miles and in some places rose to a height of twenty feet.

Above and below. The transformation wrought by the Widening is forcefully illustrated by a comparison of these two views - the first is dated 10 September 1931 and the second 19 April 1934. A footpath crossed the old GE main line by Thrift Wood (some distance west of Shenfield station, at approximately MP19¹/₂) in a curious zigzag fashion. This could not be countenanced in the new main line and this wonderful footbridge was put up as replacement. Ballast used in the Widening was crushed flint (which must have made for some incredibly sharp edges) laid over a six inch blanket of ashes. Sir Robert McAlpine, the main contractor, 'showed much energy and resource by the employment of the latest types of mechanical plant, some of the machines being specially designed for the work.' Fifty petrol tractors, 300 tip wagons, seven mechanical navvies, 23 cranes and 15 miles of temporary railway line were in service at one point - the whole project absorbed 1,450 tons of steelwork and employed an average of a thousand men. The relief of unemployment, after all, was a principal aim of the Act under which the Widening took place....

Above. Shenfield station on 10 September 1931, before the Widening. This is looking to the east; the engine turntable lies out of sight to the right.

Below. Bridge 127 and Shenfield station, down side (station master's house alongside) on 10 September 1931 - a scene, no doubt, to bring the jaw dropping of anyone who knows the place now.

Above. There were various extensions made to the goods yard at Shenfield. The short siding with buffer stops and the road on which the vehicle stands were new, as was the new-laid cart road in between.

Below. A transformed Bridge 127 (compare with photograph below left) over Billericay Road, in January 1934. It illustrates the fact that the widening here was carried out on the down (nearest) side.

Above. The new Shenfield platforms with their 'neat form of electric light', 27 March 1934. View is to the east, from the island platform, which was formerly the site of the down platform. It was lengthened to 600 feet and a new (600 feet) down platform (on the left) was built. The old up platform, over on the right out of this picture, was lengthened to 620 feet. At Shenfield the subway was lengthened to connect the new platform arrangement and luggage hoists were installed.

Below. The Shenfield block on 1 March 1934. It was regarded as somewhat utilitarian at the time, owing a little perhaps to *Art Deco* but otherwise pretty unmemorable. *The Railway Gazette* called the Shenfield block 'handsome' which is a perfectly fair description. The line was on an embankment through Shenfield and the platform level structures behind the main edifice were carried on arching.

WAY IN and WAY OUT at Shenfield, 27 March 1934.

Above. The grand edifice at Shenfield, 1 March 1934.

Left. The main entrance, 27 March 1934, and a perfect finale to this little look at a little known railway project. The term 'Widening' never sounds like much but it can, as in this case, mask a truly stupendous undertaking. A succession of ramshackle stations and a thoroughly nineteenth century main line were transformed and modernised out of all recognition. On this new main line was the Great Eastern carried forward to the electric age.